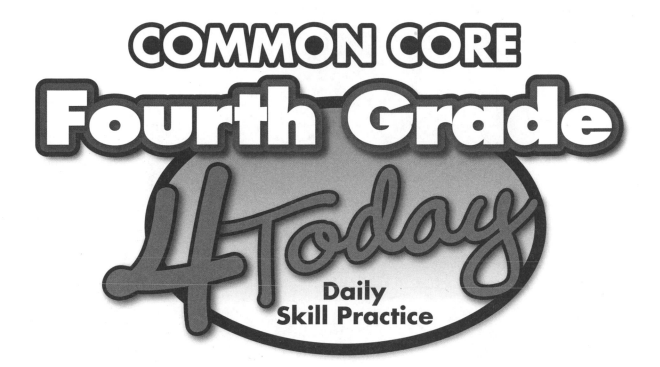

COMMON CORE
Fourth Grade
4 Today
Daily Skill Practice

Grade 4

Carson-Dellosa Publishing, LLC
Greensboro, North Carolina

Credits

Content Editors: Elise Craver, Christine Schwab, Angela Triplett
Proofreader: Karen Seberg

Carson-Dellosa Publishing, LLC
PO Box 35665
Greensboro, NC 27425 USA
carsondellosa.com

ISBN 978-1-4838-1238-0
03-287151151

Table of Contents

Introduction

Common Core Fourth Grade 4 Today is a perfect supplement to the fourth-grade classroom curriculum. Students' skills will grow as they support their knowledge of math, language arts, science, and social studies with a variety of engaging activities.

This book covers 40 weeks of daily practice. Each day will provide students with cross-curricular content practice. During the course of four days, students complete questions and activities in math, language arts, science, and social studies in about 10 minutes. On the fifth day of each week, students complete a writing assessment that corresponds with one of the week's activities.

Various skills and concepts in math and English language arts are reinforced throughout the book through activities that align to the Common Core State Standards. The standards covered for the whole week are noted at the bottom of that week's assessment page. For an overview of the standards covered, please see the Common Core State Standards Alignment Matrix on pages 5–8.

Indicates the weekly practice page

Indicates the daily practice problems

Indicates the weekly assessment

Indicates the Common Core State Standards covered in the weekly assessment

Language Arts

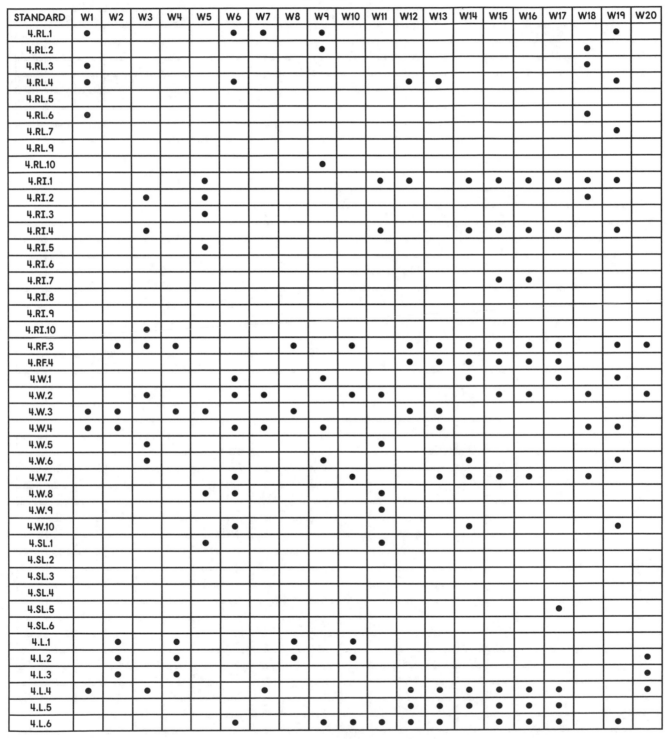

STANDARD	W1	W2	W3	W4	W5	W6	W7	W8	W9	W10	W11	W12	W13	W14	W15	W16	W17	W18	W19	W20
4.RL.1	•					•	•		•										•	
4.RL.2									•									•		
4.RL.3	•																	•		
4.RL.4	•					•						•	•						•	
4.RL.5																				
4.RL.6	•																	•		
4.RL.7																			•	
4.RL.9																				
4.RL.10									•											
4.RI.1					•						•	•		•	•	•	•	•	•	
4.RI.2			•		•													•		
4.RI.3					•															
4.RI.4			•									•		•	•	•	•		•	
4.RI.5					•															
4.RI.6																				
4.RI.7														•	•					
4.RI.8																				
4.RI.9																				
4.RI.10			•																	
4.RF.3		•	•	•				•		•		•	•	•	•	•	•		•	•
4.RF.4												•	•	•	•	•	•			
4.W.1						•			•					•			•		•	
4.W.2			•			•	•			•	•				•	•		•		•
4.W.3	•	•		•	•			•				•	•							
4.W.4	•	•				•	•		•				•					•	•	
4.W.5			•								•									
4.W.6			•						•						•				•	
4.W.7						•				•			•	•	•	•		•		
4.W.8					•	•					•									
4.W.9											•									
4.W.10						•								•					•	
4.SL.1					•						•									
4.SL.2																				
4.SL.3																				
4.SL.4																				
4.SL.5																	•			
4.SL.6																				
4.L.1		•		•				•		•										
4.L.2		•		•				•		•										•
4.L.3		•		•																•
4.L.4	•		•				•					•	•	•	•	•	•			•
4.L.5												•	•	•	•	•	•			
4.L.6						•			•	•	•	•	•		•	•	•		•	

W = Week

Common Core State Standards Alignment Matrix

Language Arts

STANDARD	W21	W22	W23	W24	W25	W26	W27	W28	W29	W30	W31	W32	W33	W34	W35	W36	W37	W38	W39	W40
4.RL.1		●						●	●											
4.RL.2									●											
4.RL.3																				
4.RL.4		●						●												
4.RL.5																				
4.RL.6																				
4.RL.7		●																		
4.RL.9																				
4.RL.10																				
4.RI.1	●	●	●	●	●	●	●	●		●		●	●	●	●	●		●	●	
4.RI.2	●			●	●	●	●					●				●		●	●	
4.RI.3				●	●	●	●					●								
4.RI.4	●	●												●	●			●		
4.RI.5				●	●	●	●												●	
4.RI.6																				
4.RI.7						●						●				●		●		
4.RI.8											●									
4.RI.9																				
4.RI.10															●					
4.RF.3	●	●	●							●	●		●					●		
4.RF.4	●			●	●		●	●	●	●		●		●	●	●		●	●	
4.W.1											●			●						
4.W.2			●		●			●	●			●		●	●	●			●	
4.W.3	●	●		●		●	●				●		●				●	●		●
4.W.4	●		●		●	●	●						●	●	●		●		●	
4.W.5		●			●				●		●									
4.W.6																			●	
4.W.7				●				●								●				
4.W.8		●																		
4.W.9																				
4.W.10	●																			
4.SL.1																				
4.SL.2																				
4.SL.3																				
4.SL.4																				
4.SL.5																				
4.SL.6																				
4.L.1											●		●				●			●
4.L.2			●								●		●				●			●
4.L.3			●														●			●
4.L.4		●	●							●	●		●	●	●	●	●	●		●
4.L.5											●							●		
4.L.6	●	●								●	●		●				●			●

W = Week

Math

STANDARD	W1	W2	W3	W4	W5	W6	W7	W8	W9	W10	W11	W12	W13	W14	W15	W16	W17	W18	W19	W20
4.OA.A.1																				
4.OA.A.2									●				●						●	●
4.OA.B.3																●				
4.OA.B.4			●	●				●		●	●				●		●			
4.OA.C.5					●		●	●								●				
4.NBT.A.1	●									●										●
4.NBT.A.2	●		●		●		●	●	●				●		●		●		●	●
4.NBT.A.3		●	●			●						●								
4.NBT.B.4		●		●	●	●		●	●		●	●	●	●				●		
4.NBT.B.5			●	●							●	●	●	●	●	●	●		●	●
4.NBT.B.6														●				●		
4.NF.A.1						●														
4.NF.A.2																				
4.NF.B.3																				
4.NF.B.4																				
4.NF.C.5																				
4.NF.C.6																				
4.NF.C.7																				
4.MD.A.1																				
4.MD.A.2																				
4.MD.A.3											●	●	●		●		●		●	
4.MD.B.4																				
4.MD.C.5																				
4.MD.C.6																				
4.MD.C.7																				
4.G.A.1																				
4.G.A.2																				
4.G.A.3																				

W = Week

Common Core State Standards Alignment Matrix

Math

STANDARD	W21	W22	W23	W24	W25	W26	W27	W28	W29	W30	W31	W32	W33	W34	W35	W36	W37	W38	W39	W40
4.OA.A.1														●						
4.OA.A.2	●									●		●								●
4.OA.B.3					●				●						●					
4.OA.B.4			●			●											●			
4.OA.C.5			●																	
4.NBT.A.1																				
4.NBT.A.2																				
4.NBT.A.3								●												
4.NBT.B.4																				
4.NBT.B.5		●					●													
4.NBT.B.6				●							●				●			●		
4.NF.A.1																				
4.NF.A.2				●		●	●													
4.NF.B.3	●	●	●	●	●			●				●								●
4.NF.B.4						●			●	●				●						
4.NF.C.5																				
4.NF.C.6		●	●	●			●	●	●	●						●				
4.NF.C.7							●											●		
4.MD.A.1											●							●		●
4.MD.A.2																	●			
4.MD.A.3		●																		
4.MD.B.4																			●	
4.MD.C.5																				
4.MD.C.6												●		●	●	●				
4.MD.C.7																	●			
4.G.A.1										●		●								
4.G.A.2												●				●				●
4.G.A.3													●							

W = Week

CD-104821 • © Carson-Dellosa

1. Write the number in standard form.

   60,000 + 5,000 + 300 + 3 _____

2. How many more students voted for baseball and basketball than football?

   _____

3. 20 ÷ 2 = _____

Favorite Sports

Trey and Nick were roller-skating down the sidewalk. Nick hit a stone and fell. His knees and hands slammed into the ground. It was a good thing he was wearing kneepads. His hands were another story.

1. Circle two words in the paragraph that start with a silent consonant.

2. What is another word that you could use instead of **slammed**? _____

3. What was the effect of Nick hitting a stone while roller-skating? _____

   _____

4. What happened to Nick's hands? _____

Write the name of a science tool to correctly complete each sentence.

1. Tia measures the height of a small houseplant with a _____.

2. Carlos uses a _____ to see if the water is hot enough.

3. Kim finds the mass of a rock using a _____.

4. Lily uses a _____ to measure six milliliters of water.

5. Ty watches the minute and second hands on the _____ to find out how long it takes the ice cube to melt.

Citizens have basic rights, such as freedom of speech, that are protected by law. Citizens also have responsibilities. As a citizen, a person must obey the laws and show respect for other people's rights, even if he does not agree with them.

1. Fill in the chart with your rights and responsibilities as a citizen of your school.

Rights	Responsibilities

Name_____

Imagine that you are an athletic superstar. What sport would you play? How would your life change? Would you spend your money on fancy things or donate your money to charity? Write an imaginary narrative with at least two paragraphs about your life as an athletic superstar. Include details to describe thoughts, feelings, or actions.

_____

_____

_____

_____

_____

_____

_____

_____

_____

_____

_____

_____

_____

_____

_____

_____

_____

_____

_____

_____

_____

_____

_____

_____

 4.RL.1, 4.RL.3, 4.RL.4, 4.RL.6, 4.W.3, 4.W.4, 4.L.4, 4.NBT.A.1, 4.NBT.A.2   CD-104821 • © Carson-Dellosa

Name_____

1. 45,678 + 21,456 = _____

2. What is the value of the following coins? _____

    2 quarters, 4 dimes, and 6 pennies

3. What is the name of the figure shown?

    _____

4. Round 54,878 to the nearest ten thousand. _____

Use proofreading marks to correct the capitalization errors.

1. Did you watch the rose parade on new year's eve?

Fill in the blank with the correct form of the verb **to be** (is, am, are).

2. I _____ going to the movies on Saturday.

Add the correct punctuation mark to the end of the sentence.

3. Do you want to go to the movies on Saturday night ____

Write the plural form of the following nouns.

4. tooth _____   woman _____   mouse _____

1. What measurement system is used in the science community?

    _____

2. Why do all scientists use this system?

    _____

    _____

    _____

If someone has power, he can direct or control a person or thing. If someone has authority, she has been given the right to have and use power. Authority is given to someone through customs, laws, or consent.

1. Explain why your teacher has the authority to tell his students to work quietly.

    _____

    _____

2. Explain why a police officer has the authority to write a speeding ticket to someone who is driving faster than the speed limit.

    _____

    _____

A popular saying says, "Don't rain on my parade." What do you think this means? Give an example of a time when somebody "rained on your parade." Write a personal narrative with at least two paragraphs about a time when your plans were spoiled or did not work out as expected. Include details to describe thoughts, feelings, or actions. Provide a concluding statement.

_____

_____

_____

_____

_____

_____

_____

_____

_____

_____

_____

_____

_____

_____

_____

_____

_____

_____

_____

_____

_____

_____

_____

_____

4.RF.3, 4.W.3, 4.W.4, 4.L.1, 4.L.2, 4.L.3, 4.NBT.A.3, 4.NBT.B.4 CD-104821 • © Carson-Dellosa

1. Write **<**, **>**, or **=** to make the statement true.

   17,987 ◯ 17,877

2. 20 × 5 = _____   20 × 6 = _____   20 × 7 = _____

3. Round each number to the nearest ten. Then, add.

   34 + 81 is about _____.

4. List the factors of 12. _____

   Is this number prime or composite? _____

The Richter Scale was developed by Charles Richter. It compares the size of earthquakes. The scale tells us how big or serious an earthquake is. This is the earthquake's **magnitude**. A magnitude of 4.0–4.9 means people can feel the earthquake, but it does little damage. A magnitude of 6.0–6.9 means that the earthquake can cause a great deal of damage in a large area.

1. Circle each word that has three or more syllables.

2. What does **magnitude** mean? _____

3. What is the effect of a magnitude 4.5 earthquake? _____

4. What does it mean as the numbers get higher? _____

Draw a line to match each science process skill with its definition.

1. observing   A. grouping objects based on characteristics or qualities

2. classifying   B. using your five senses to learn about the world

3. communicating   C. telling how objects are alike and different

4. inferring   D. making an educated guess about what will happen

5. predicting   E. sharing information using words and visual aids

6. comparing   F. using what you know and learn to make conclusions

The **Bill of Rights** is the name of the first 10 amendments to the Constitution. The founding fathers added this section that describes the basic rights and freedoms of American citizens. Read the statements relating to the amendments in the Bill of Rights. Write **T** if it is true or **F** if it is false.

1. _____ The government can make it illegal to speak your opinion.

2. _____ The government can tell the media which stories they can cover.

3. _____ Citizens can gather in meetings as long as they are peaceful.

4. _____ No one can take away your property without legal permission.

5. _____ A person cannot be sent to trial without a cause.

Name_____

Six science process skills are observing, classifying, communicating, inferring, predicting, and comparing. Write an informative essay about conducting a science experiment. It can be an experiment you have done in the past or one you would like to try. Describe your hypothesis and the steps to conducting your experiment. Be sure to use each of the science process skills in your explanation. Show your essay to your teacher. Make changes if needed. Then, type your report on a computer.

_____

_____

_____

_____

_____

_____

_____

_____

_____

_____

_____

_____

_____

_____

_____

_____

_____

_____

_____

_____

_____

_____

_____

 4.RI.2, 4.RI.4, 4.RI.10, 4.RF.3, 4.W.2, 4.W.5, 4.W.6, 4.L.4, 4.OA.B.4, 4.NBT.A.2, 4.NBT.A.3, 4.NBT.B.5   CD-104821 • © Carson-Dellosa

Name_____

1. 2,535 − 2,172 = _____

2. 5 × 3 = 15

   Write a related multiplication fact. _____

3. 30 × 2 = _____   30 × 3 = _____   30 × 4 = _____

4. List the factors of 11. _____

   Is this number prime or composite? _____

Use proofreading marks to correct the capitalization errors.

1. The class planted a tree on arbor day.

Fill in the blank with the correct form of the verb **to be** (is, am, are).

2. You _____ a nice person.

Add the correct punctuation mark to the end of the sentence.

3. What do you like to eat at the movies _____

Write the plural form of the following nouns.

4. ox _____   moose _____   fish _____

Write **true** or **false**.

1. _____ The problem is always stated as a question.

2. _____ The experiment's conclusion and its hypothesis are always the same.

3. _____ The hypothesis is the final answer in an experiment.

4. _____ Scientists do not like to share the results of their experiments.

5. _____ When scientists interpret the data, they decide what the information means.

Rules and laws are necessary for a community to run smoothly. Having rules and laws makes citizens feel safe and secure. The government works to keep order and discourage violence. Write what you think would happen if the following rules and laws did not exist.

1. Traffic laws _____

   _____

2. Right to a trial by jury _____

   _____

3. Right to private property _____

   _____

Name_____

Imagine your principal has decided there will not be any rules to follow at school for the day. Write a journal entry that describes the kind of day you would have at school without rules. Include dialogue and details to describe thoughts, feelings, or actions. Provide a concluding statement.

_____

_____

_____

_____

_____

_____

_____

_____

_____

_____

_____

_____

_____

_____

_____

_____

_____

_____

_____

_____

_____

_____

_____

_____

4.RF.3, 4.W.3, 4.L.1, 4.L.2, 4.L.3, 4.OA.B.4, 4.NBT.B.4, 4.NBT.B.5

Name_____

1. 66,859 – 34,437 = _____

2. Write **<**, **>**, or **=** to make the statement true.

3. Complete the related multiplication facts.

    32 ÷ 4   20 ÷ 5   24 ÷ 6

    4 × _____   5 × _____   6 × _____

4. Determine the 18th shape in the pattern. _____

    △ □ ○

The Underground Railroad was not a railroad at all. But, like a train ride, the Underground Railroad moved people along. Those who escaped often followed routes that had been laid out by others before them. However, unlike a train ride, some routes went underground through dirt tunnels without any sort of tracks.

1. What two things does this paragraph compare? _____

2. How is the subject like the thing it is compared with? _____

3. How is the subject unlike the thing it is compared with? _____

4. How does this paragraph make you feel? _____

    _____

---

1. Nora believes that the scientific method is the only way to carry out scientific inquiry. Do you agree? Why or why not? Give examples to support your point of view.

    _____

    _____

    _____

    _____

A **primary source** is a document or physical object, which was written or created during the time in which you are studying. A **secondary source** interprets and analyzes primary sources. Secondary sources contain pictures, quotes, or graphics of primary sources.

1. Look at the list of sources. Write **P** if the object is a primary source. Write **S** if it is a secondary source.

    _____ diary   _____ newspaper

    _____ encyclopedia   _____ original art

    _____ letters   _____ textbook

Name_____

If you could go back in time for one hour, would you? Think about your life five years or eight years ago. Can you remember a special time that you would like to live over again? What happened? Is there anything that you would do differently this time? Why is this memory important to you? Write an essay. Include details to describe thoughts, feelings, or actions.

_____

_____

_____

_____

_____

_____

_____

_____

_____

_____

_____

_____

_____

_____

_____

_____

_____

_____

_____

_____

_____

_____

_____

_____

4.RI.1, 4.RI.2, 4.RI.3, 4.RI.5, 4.W.3, 4.W.8, 4.SL.1, 4.OA.C.5, 4.NBT.A.2, 4.NBT.B.4

Name_____

1. Round 7,667 to the nearest hundred. _____

2. Divide the rectangle into sixths.
   Label each sixth with an appropriate fraction.

3. Oliver earns $4 a day for 7 days for doing chores. Each day, his mom takes out $2 and puts it into a savings account for Oliver. How much money does Oliver get to keep after 7 days? _____

4. $8,987 – $8,765 = _____

One day, Jimmy raced into the kitchen and announced, "I am no longer eating anything green! I just found out that all green food was developed to turn humans into aliens. So, I won't be able to eat anything like peas or broccoli!"

"I'm so sorry to hear that, Jimmy," replied his mom. "I guess you won't be having any key lime pie or mint chocolate chip ice cream for dessert tonight."

1. Circle all of the words that have the same vowel sound as **meat/meet**.

2. What word could you use instead of **announced**? _____

3. How might Jimmy react to his mother's comment? _____

4. Why did Jimmy say that all green food was developed to turn humans into aliens?
   _____

Label each statement **O** for observation or **I** for inference.

1. _____ The mealworms moved toward the light source.

2. _____ Warming eggs with red light helps the chicks inside grow better.

3. _____ Soap bubbles made with glycerin pop an average of four seconds after the normal bubbles.

4. _____ Water from source B is cloudy and has sediment in it.

5. _____ Cold temperatures cause candy with a lot of sugar to shatter more easily.

Cities provide many services to their citizens. The **mayor** and **city council** make the rules that everyone must follow. They also discuss community issues, such as whether to build a new library or park. City employees include police officers and firefighters. City services include the water and electricity companies. Some cities have special programs such as library reading clubs or computer classes for senior citizens.

1. Name two employees who work for the city. _____

2. What do the mayor and city council members do? _____
   _____

3. How can people help their community? _____
   _____

If there were one food you could keep off your dinner plate forever, what would it be? Write a short essay to tell why you don't like it. Use sensory words such as **taste**, **feel**, **smell**, or **look**. Then, use the Internet or books to find out more about the food. Is there something good or special about the food? Does this change your mind about eating it? Add the new information to your original essay. Separate the essay into paragraphs. Include facts and definitions to explain or inform.

_____

_____

_____

_____

_____

_____

_____

_____

_____

_____

_____

_____

_____

_____

_____

_____

_____

_____

_____

_____

_____

_____

_____

4.RL.1, 4.RL.4, 4.W.1, 4.W.2, 4.W.4, 4.W.7, 4.W.8, 4.W.10, 4.L.6, 4.NBT.A.3, 4.NBT.B.4, 4.NF.A.1

1. Fill in the missing numbers to complete the pattern.

   615, 605, 595, _____ , _____ , _____

2. How many inches long is the feather?

   _____

3. Write **<**, **>**, or **=** to make the statement true.   121,453 ◯ 112,678

"Let's clean up," said Mrs. Perez. "It's nearly time to go home." Andre hurried to the pet corner to take care of the hamster. Just as he was fastening the door to the hamster cage, the fire alarm rang. The teacher and children quickly left the building. The hamster looked at the half-closed door.

1. What two words form each contraction in the passage? _____ _____
2. Give a word other than **hurried** that describes moving quickly. _____
3. Try to predict what happens. Does the hamster
   A. close the door?   B. escape?   C. go to sleep?
4. What clues helped you answer question 3? _____
   _____

1. What is **matter**?
   _____
   _____

2. Think about an orange. Describe four of its physical properties.
   _____
   _____
   _____

A famous quote from the Declaration of Independence states: *We hold these truths to be self-evident, that all men are created equal, that they are endowed by their Creator with certain unalienable Rights, that among these are Life, Liberty and the pursuit of Happiness.*

1. List ways you enjoy the rights of life, liberty, and happiness. _____
   _____
   _____

2. How does the government protect these rights? _____
   _____
   _____

Matter is anything that takes up state and has mass. Depending on your age, this might be difficult to understand. Imagine that you are a kindergarten teacher. Think of an easy way to explain what matter is to six-year-old children. Use easy and descriptive words. Use objects to help with your explanation. Write an essay about what you would say, do, and show. Then, show the essay to your teacher. Make changes if needed.

_____

_____

_____

_____

_____

_____

_____

_____

_____

_____

_____

_____

_____

_____

_____

_____

_____

_____

_____

_____

_____

_____

_____

4.RL.1, 4.W.2, 4.W.4, 4.L.4, 4.OA.C.5, 4.NBT.A.2

1.   List the factors of 14. _____

     Is this number prime or composite? _____

2.   Write **<**, **>**, or **=** to make each statement true.

     315 ◯ 415   649 ◯ 694   5,874 ◯ 5,784

3.   Fill in the missing numbers to complete the pattern.

     145, 148, 151, _____ , _____ , _____

Use proofreading marks to correct the capitalization errors.

1.   The Iroquois lived in the mountains of new york and pennsylvania.

Write the correct word (their, there, they're) in the blank.

2.   _____ homes were in the mountains.

Add the missing commas.

3.   Famous tribes include the Iroquois the Ojibwa the Lakota and the Nez Percé tribes.

Make the verbs past tense. **Example**: tip = tipped

4.   stop _____ wag _____ hum _____

Write **P** if the example is a physical change. Write **C** if the example is a chemical change.

1.   _____ cutting a smaller slice of bread

2.   _____ burning wood

3.   _____ adding water to soup

4.   _____ a car fender rusting

5.   _____ ice melting

6.   _____ an avocado browning

7.   _____ crushing a can

8.   _____ stapling paper together

9.   _____ dissolving sugar in tea

10. _____ melting silver

Diplomats are people from different countries that work together to try to solve conflicts between nations. Diplomacy involves agreements and compromises from all countries involved in the conflict. Leaders from each country sign a treaty when they feel the dispute has been settled fairly. Circle the best ending to each sentence.

1.   If you use diplomacy, you will _____.

     A. solve conflicts peacefully   B. make enemies

2.   If you are a diplomatic person, you _____.

     A. try to avoid conflict   B. try to create conflict

Name_____

Think of a time you were involved in a dispute or had a conflict with someone. What happened? How was the conflict or dispute finally settled? Was it settled fairly? If it wasn't, could you have done anything differently to change the outcome? Write a narrative about a time you had a disagreement with someone. Include dialogue and details to describe thoughts, feelings, or actions.

_____
_____
_____
_____
_____
_____
_____
_____
_____
_____
_____
_____
_____
_____
_____
_____
_____
_____
_____
_____
_____
_____
_____
_____

4.RF.3, 4.W.3, 4.L.1, 4.L.2, 4.OA.B.4, 4.OA.C.5, 4.NBT.A.2, 4.NBT.B.4

1. Write the number word as a number.

   ninety-five thousand one hundred seventy-five _____

2. Leo has 24 golf clubs. He has 3 golf bags. Each bag contains the same number of clubs. How many golf clubs are in each bag? _____

3. Show how to solve this problem.

   5 × 5 × 4 =

4. Last year, Langdon School had $127,657 available for scholarships. This year, the school has $141,509 available. How much more money does the school have for scholarships this year? _____

You would never believe what I saw tonight. We were by the Congress Avenue Bridge. As the sun was going down, I saw a cloud moving around by the bridge. The cloud was made up of bats! The bats live under the bridge where it is dark. The sun does not shine under the bridge, but when the sun started to go down, the bats woke up.

1. Where is the author of this passage? _____

   _____

2. What is the thing the author is reporting? _____

3. Does the author sound **amazed** or **unexcited**? _____

4. Did you learn any more about what time it is? If so, what? _____

   _____

Draw a line to match each term with its meaning.

1. energy   A. the energy of an object because it is moving

2. potential energy   B. the energy caused by a chemical change

3. kinetic energy   C. the ability to do work

4. mechanical energy   D. the energy of motion

5. electrical energy   E. the energy that an object has because of its position

6. chemical energy   F. the energy caused by the flow of electricity

Homes and home life have changed over time. Many of the changes have occurred because of advances in technology. The refrigerator, washing machine, television, and electric light are some examples. Automobiles and airplanes have changed how people travel.

1. Choose an item from the passage. Describe how advances in technology have changed that item over time.

   _____

   _____

Name_____

Imagine you have been invited to attend a summer golf camp with many fun activities. There are only a limited number of spaces available. The application requires you to include an essay. The essay should tell four reasons why you deserve to be chosen to attend the camp. Write an essay with four short paragraphs. Show it to your teacher. Make changes if needed. Then, type it on a computer.

_____
_____
_____
_____
_____
_____
_____
_____
_____
_____
_____
_____
_____
_____
_____
_____
_____
_____
_____
_____
_____
_____
_____
_____
_____
_____
_____
_____

4.RL.1, 4.RL.2, 4.RL.10, 4.W.1, 4.W.4, 4.W.6, 4.L.6, 4.OA.A.2, 4.NBT.A.2, 4.NBT.B.4

1. List the factors of 20. _____

   Is this number prime or composite? _____

2. What is the perimeter of the shape? _____

   1 cm   6 cm
   4 cm   4 cm
      3 cm   2 cm

3. Are these fractions equivalent fractions?

   _____

4. 10,000 ÷ 1,000 = _____

Day 1

Use proofreading marks to correct the capitalization errors.

1. The city of cheyenne was named for the Tribe that lived in wyoming.

Write the correct word (their, there, they're) in the blank.

2. _____ were many Cheyenne tribes in Wyoming.

Add the missing comma.

3. A Native American burial mound is near the town of Aberdeen Ohio.

Make the verbs past tense. **Example**: cry = cried

4. try _____   hurry _____   study _____

Day 2

---

1. How does energy change when you turn on a lamp?

   _____

   _____

   _____

2. How does energy change when you eat food?

   _____

   _____

   _____

Day 3

Draw a line to match each word to its definition.

1. generation   A. a relative from long ago

2. heritage   B. a group of people born and living at the same time

3. ancestor   C. something attained from the past

4. tradition   D. a belief or custom handed down across generations

5. Describe a tradition that you and your family have. _____

Day 4

Name_____

How much do you know about American Indian tribes? Choose one to write about. Use the Internet, books, or magazines to find more information about this tribe. Take notes about what you learn. Be sure to include information about the tribe's history, beliefs, and traditions. Include facts and definitions to explain or inform. Then, add an illustration to your report by drawing and coloring the tribe's flag.

_____

_____

_____

_____

_____

_____

_____

_____

_____

_____

_____

_____

_____

_____

_____

_____

4.RF.3, 4.W.2, 4.W.7, 4.L.1, 4.L.2, 4.L.6, 4.OA.B.4, 4.NBT.A.1

1. Paige saw 142 tourists in May, June, and July. She saw 32 tourists in May and 89 tourists in June. How many tourists did Paige see in July? _____

2. List the factors of 79. _____

   Is this number prime or composite? _____

3. 97,808 − 31,876 = _____

4. Find the area of the rectangle. _____

10 m

7 m

Day 1

A **fierce** warrior, Crazy Horse was known as a Lakota tribe member who would not give up. Born in 1849, Crazy Horse worked hard to keep the Native American way of life from disappearing. He did not want to lose the customs of his tribe.

1. Write **would not** as a contraction. _____

2. What does **fierce** mean? _____

3. Why did the author write this paragraph? _____

   _____

4. What did Crazy Horse work hard to do? _____

   _____

Day 2

Write the word that completes each sentence.

1. A leaf falls off a tree because of the force of _____.

2. A soccer ball slows down and stops rolling because of the force of _____.

3. A book will stay on a table until it is picked up because of _____.

Answer the question. Then, discuss your answer with a partner.

4. How would you explain to your friend why it is harder to walk up the stairs than to walk down them? _____

   _____

Day 3

The Plains Indians used tepees for homes. They were made of buffalo hide and wooden poles. Tepees had an open space at the top to allow for a small fire in the center for cooking and warmth. The men would often paint symbols of their achievements on the outside.

1. Draw a tepee using details from the passage.

Day 4

Sir Isaac Newton was a scientist who studied the movement of objects. He proposed three laws of motion. The first law states that any object in motion will continue to move unless forces act on it. The second law says that the greater the mass of an object, the more force it will take to accelerate it. The last law of motion says that for every action, there is an equal and opposite reaction. Write a report about one of the laws of motion. Use books and the Internet to find more information. Summarize what you have learned. Include examples in your writing. Then, read your report to two other students. Ask them if they understand the law of motion you described. Make changes if needed.

_____
_____
_____
_____
_____
_____
_____
_____
_____
_____
_____
_____
_____
_____
_____
_____
_____
_____
_____
_____
_____
_____
_____

4.RI.1, 4.RI.4, 4.W.2, 4.W.5, 4.W.8, 4.W.9, 4.SL.1, 4.L.6, 4.OA.B.4, 4.NBT.B.4, 4.MD.A.3

1. The area of a window measures 336 square inches.
    If the window is 16 inches wide, how long is the window? _____

2. 73,461 – 3,861 = _____

3. Round 438,692 to the nearest thousand. _____

4. 41 × 6 = _____

Demetri came down with the flu on Monday night, and his doctor told him to stay home from school for the rest of the week. She told him that he could do schoolwork on Thursday, but not to **overdo** it.

1. **Over-** is a prefix that means "too much" or "more than usual." So, what does **overdo** mean? _____

2. Circle the phrase that matches the doctor's advice to Demetri: "Do schoolwork, but take it easy," or "Be sure to do all of your schoolwork."

3. How many days was Demetri home not doing schoolwork? _____

4. Is having the flu an excuse to ignore your schoolwork? _____
    _____

Label the diagram.

5. What does the diagram show?
    _____

In 1620, the *Mayflower* traveled for 66 days across the Atlantic Ocean. It carried 102 passengers and almost 30 crewmembers. Travel was difficult. The weather was often stormy and made the seas rough. Passengers ate oatmeal, hard biscuits, dried fruit, and salted beef they had brought with them from England. Many passengers became seasick during the trip.

1. How was the trip on the *Mayflower* different from a trip on a big ship today?
    _____
    _____
    _____

Name_____

Imagine leaving behind your home and all your things to sail across the ocean to a new world where there are no towns and no homes. Imagine you are one of the passengers on the *Mayflower*. Write a letter home to your best friend in England. Describe your voyage on the *Mayflower*. Describe the food, the weather, and how you are spending your time on the ship. Write your thoughts on what the new world will be like when you finally arrive.

_____
_____
_____
_____
_____
_____
_____
_____
_____
_____
_____
_____
_____
_____
_____
_____
_____
_____
_____
_____
_____
_____
_____
_____
_____

4.RL.4, 4.RI.1, 4.RF.3, 4.RF.4, 4.W.3, 4.L.4, 4.L.5, 4.L.6, 4.NBT.A.3, 4.NBT.B.4, 4.NBT.B.5, 4.MD.A.3

CD-104821 • © Carson-Dellosa

Day 1

1. 232 × 4 = _____

2. 183,982 + 81,294 = _____

3. Write the number word as a number.

   seventeen thousand four hundred thirty-three _____

4. Write the equation.

   Melanie bought 7 packages of greeting cards. Each package had 9 cards. How many greeting cards did she get in all? _____

Day 2

Jose and Gabby needed information for their report on theropods. It was hard to find **resources** on this dinosaur. They decided not to get another topic. They would leave no stone unturned while looking for information.

1. Circle all of the words with three syllables.

2. What are **resources**? _____

3. Are theropods common dinosaurs to study? What detail helps you answer that question? _____

4. What does "leave no stone unturned" mean? Will they turn over every stone they see to look for theropod fossils, or will they look for information everywhere? _____

Day 3

1. The ends of the magnets are called _____.

2. There is a north end and a _____ end.

3. If a magnet is tied to a string and held in the air, the north end of the magnet will point _____.

4. The unlike ends of two magnets _____ each other.

5. The like ends of two magnets _____ each other.

Day 4

Draw a line to match each word to its definition.

1. pioneer   A. someone who lives in a particular place

2. migration   B. the first settler in a region

3. territory   C. an area of land

4. inhabitant   D. the act of moving from one place to another

5. Write a complete sentence using one of the words from the list.

   _____

   _____

Do you have a job or some way to earn extra money? Believe it or not, jobs can be found at any age. They may be small after-school jobs like mowing a neighbor's lawn or delivering newspapers. What are some other ways someone your age can earn money? Find out more by asking your classmates about their job experience. Write an essay on this topic, including personal experience. Organize it by using paragraphs.

_____

_____

_____

_____

_____

_____

_____

_____

_____

_____

_____

_____

_____

_____

_____

_____

_____

_____

_____

_____

_____

_____

_____

_____

_____

4.RL.4, 4.RF.3, 4.RF.4, 4.W.3, 4.W.4, 4.W.7, 4.L.4, 4.L.5, 4.L.6, 4.OA.A.2, 4.NBT.A.2, 4.NBT.B.4, 4.NBT.B.5, 4.MD.A.3
CD-104821 • © Carson-Dellosa

Day 1

1. 147 × 2 = _____

2. 67,987 – 32,998 = _____

3. 500 ÷ 50 = _____

4. A rectangular closet has a perimeter of 10 feet. If the width of the closet is 3 feet, what is the length of the closet? _____

Day 2

A tarantula is a big, hairy spider. You might have seen one in a pet shop that carries spiders and other unusual pets. In the United States, tarantulas live in the West, where it is hot and dry. During the day, tarantulas sleep in holes and other dark places. They come out at night to hunt for food.

1. What word has a **t** that is pronounced like **ch**? _____

2. Write antonyms for **big** and **hairy**. _____

3. If you visit a pet shop that carries unusual pets, what pet might you see?

   A. cat   B. canary   C. tarantula

4. What might happen if you stuck your hand in a dark hole in Arizona? _____
   _____

Day 3

Unscramble the letters in parentheses to complete each sentence with a device that uses electromagnetism.

1. Some _____ (ordo scolk) need an electrical signal to unlock and open.

2. Some _____(ardh ridesv) in computers use electromagnetism to store and retrieve information.

3. When the power goes out, many homes and businesses use _____(retgneasro) to produce electricity.

4. Special _____(rcnaes) in junkyards can pick up and separate the metal objects from other trash.

Day 4

The Fountain of Youth was supposed to be on an island called Bimini. A Spanish explorer, named Ponce de León, wanted to find it. He was getting old and the water from the magical fountain would make him young forever. In 1513, he set sail from Puerto Rico and headed northwest. A month later, he discovered a new place. He named it Florida. Believing it was an island, he tried to sail around it but the Fountain of Youth was nowhere to be found.

1. Why did Ponce de León want to find the Fountain of Youth? _____
   _____

2. What new land did he discover? _____

Some people think tarantulas are gross or scary. Other people are fascinated by them.
What do you think? Do you think a tarantula would make a good pet? Why or why not? Write
an essay explaining your opinion of tarantulas. Use the Internet, books, or magazines to find
out more about them. Include facts to support your reasons. Then, type your essay on a
computer. Share your essay with a classmate. Make changes if necessary.

_____

_____

_____

_____

_____

_____

_____

_____

_____

_____

_____

_____

_____

_____

_____

_____

_____

_____

_____

_____

_____

_____

_____

_____

**4.RI.1, 4.RI.4, 4.RF.3, 4.RF.4, 4.W.1, 4.W.6, 4.W.7, 4.W.10,
4.L.4, 4.L.5, 4.NBT.B.4, 4.NBT.B.5, 4.NBT.B.6**

1. $8,867 \times 5 =$ _____

2. Write the number word as a number.

   five thousand eight hundred ninety-two _____

3. List the factors of 68. _____

   Is this number prime or composite? _____

4. The perimeter of the top of a desk is 54 inches. If the length of the desk is 15 inches, what is the width of the desk? _____

Tarantulas catch their food mostly by jumping on it and biting it. Smaller tarantulas eat insects. Larger ones eat mice and lizards. A tarantula's poison can kill the animals it hunts, but its poison cannot kill a human.

1. Circle the word that has an ending sound like the second **t** in **tarantula**.

2. What is another word for "the animals it hunts"?

   A. prey   B. toast   C. pray

3. What information in this paragraph might make you feel better about meeting up with a tarantula? _____

4. What kills the animals a tarantula hunts? _____

1. Circle the sound wave that has a low pitch.

2. Explain why you circled the picture you did.

   _____

   _____

   _____

Early people lived as hunter-gatherers. They ate roots, seeds, and other wild plants that they had gathered. They hunted **game** for food. Many groups were nomadic and followed the animals they hunted. This way of life changed when agriculture began and people started to grow crops. Irrigation practices improved, bringing essential water to crops, and farming settlements grew.

1. What does **game** mean? _____

2. What caused the nomads' way of life to change? _____

   _____

3. Why did farming settlements start to grow? _____

   _____

Name_____

   Imagine you have been asked to build a musical instrument. Your materials are a shoebox with a hole cut into the lid and various rubber bands. Some of the rubber bands are thick and some are skinny. They are of different lengths. Describe an instrument you can make. How will you organize your rubber bands? The rubber bands will make different sounds. Explain what causes this. If you have time, make an instrument like you have described to test your theory.

_____
_____
_____
_____
_____
_____
_____
_____
_____
_____
_____
_____
_____
_____
_____
_____
_____
_____
_____
_____
_____
_____
_____
_____

 4.RI.1, 4.RI.4, 4.RI.7, 4.RF.3, 4.RF.4, 4.W.2, 4.W.7, 4.L.4, 4.L.5, 4.L.6, 4.OA.B.4, 4.NBT.A.2, 4.NBT.B.5, 4.MD.A.3   CD-104821 • © Carson-Dellosa

Day 1

1. Start at 92. Create a pattern that adds 13 to each number. Stop when you have 5 numbers. _____

2. 80 ÷ 8 = _____

3. 77 × 80 = _____

4. The movie theater had 135 people in it. If the people split into 9 even groups to watch different movies, how many people will watch each movie? _____

Day 2

If you are bitten by a tarantula, you will soon know that a bite hurts only about as much as a bee sting. Its bite helps this spider protect itself. Tarantulas are shy spiders. They bite humans only if they feel threatened and cannot get away.

1. Is the **i** sound in **bitten** a long or short vowel sound? _____

2. What is another word the author could have used instead of **shy**? _____

3. What will someone who has been bitten by a tarantula do?

   A. feel nothing   B. feel a bite like a bee sting

4. What will poking or touching a tarantula make it do?

   A. nothing   B. bite you

Day 3

1. Write a caption to support this diagram.

   _____

   _____

Day 4

The US government is divided into three branches: legislative, executive, and judicial. The legislative branch writes the laws. The executive branch carries out the laws and makes sure they are obeyed. The judicial system is given the power to interpret the laws. The three branches provide a system of **checks and balances** to help make sure that no one branch becomes too powerful.

1. What does **checks and balances** mean? _____

   _____

2. Judgments about laws are made by the _____ branch.

3. Laws are written by members of the _____ branch.

4. The _____ branch puts laws into action.

Choose one of the three branches of government. Use the Internet, books, or magazines to learn more. Write a detailed report with facts and definitions describing the function of either the executive, legislative, or judicial branch of government. Show it to your teacher. Make changes if needed. Then, type it on a computer.

_____

_____

_____

_____

_____

_____

_____

_____

_____

_____

_____

_____

_____

_____

_____

_____

_____

_____

_____

_____

_____

_____

_____

_____

_____

4.RI.1, 4.RI.4, 4.RI.7, 4.RF.3, 4.RF.4, 4.W.2, 4.W.7, 4.L.4, 4.L.5, 4.L.6, 4.OA.B.3, 4.OA.C.5, 4.NBT.B.5

1. The area of a rectangle is 1,035 square centimeters. If the length of the rectangle is 3 centimeters, what is the width of the rectangle? _____

2. Write **<**, **>**, or **=** to make the statement true.

   94,306 ◯ 94,360

3. List the factors of 75. _____

   Is this number prime or composite? _____

4. 2,002 × 4 = _____

A tarantula can bite, but has another way to protect itself. It can rub its hind legs together, which causes its stiff leg hairs to fly up in the air. Each tiny hair can make a hurtful skin or eye wound.

1. Circle all of the words that have a long **i** sound.

2. Which meaning of **wound** is correct here: **wrapped around** or **injury**?

3. What details does the writer use to describe tarantula hairs? _____

4. If you got down on your knees to look closely at a tarantula that was rubbing its hind legs together, what might happen? _____

Prepare for a presentation on plants. Label the parts of a flower. Tell what each part does. Discuss with a partner.

1. _____

2. _____

3. _____

4. _____

Britain ruled the American colonies in the 1700s. Some colonists were called **Loyalists**. They felt strong ties to Britain. But, the majority of colonists wanted liberty from the British king's laws. They created their own **militia** to combat the British troops. These colonists dreamed of a separate American nation. They were known as **Patriots**.

1. What does **militia** mean? _____

2. Explain the difference between a **Patriot** and a **Loyalist**.

   _____

   _____

Name_____

How tall are you? Imagine you are 16 feet tall. About how many times taller is that than your present height? Would you like to be 16 feet tall? How would your life change? Write an essay to explain what the world would be like if you were 16 feet tall. Include your opinion about your new height and give reasons to support it.

_____

_____

_____

_____

_____

_____

_____

_____

_____

_____

_____

_____

_____

_____

_____

_____

_____

_____

_____

_____

_____

_____

_____

_____

4.RI.1, 4.RI.4, 4.RF.3, 4.RF.4, 4.W.1, 4.SL.5, 4.L.4, 4.L.5, 4.L.6, 4.OA.B.4, 4.NBT.A.2, 4.NBT.B.5, 4.MD.A.3

Day 1

1. 728 ÷ 8 = _____

2. 624,193 + 353,126 = _____

3. 50 ÷ 5 = _____

4. Liza works 7 hours a day, 7 days a week. How many hours does Liza work in 6 weeks? _____

Day 2

"When did you get to know so much about spiders?" asked Myra.

"I just read a book about them," Dave answered. "Like insects, spiders are invertebrates. They have a hard outer shell called an exoskeleton. The exoskeleton protects the soft inside parts of their bodies. They also have special eyes that help them hunt. The part I found the most interesting is that the spider, the horseshoe crab, and the scorpion all belong to the same group."

1. How are insects and spiders similar? _____

2. How does Dave feel about spiders? _____

3. How do you feel about spiders? _____

_____

Day 3

Animals with backbones can be classified into smaller groups, or classes. Draw a line to match each class with one of its defining characteristics.

1. fish   A. feeds its young milk

2. amphibian   B. has a body covered in dry scales

3. reptile   C. lives in freshwater or salt water

4. bird   D. has a body covered in feathers

5. mammal   E. lives part of its life in the water and part of it on land

Day 4

The Chinese were the first to use and print paper money in the seventh century. A thousand years later, the Europeans began making paper money. Paper money is actually made of cloth. It is a blend of 25 percent cotton and 75 percent linen. Special inks have to be carefully mixed to create the exact colors for paper money. There are also special security threads in the bills. These threads prevent people from **counterfeiting** money.

1. What does **counterfeit** mean? _____

2. Write two facts about paper money. _____

_____

_____

Name_____

Spiders, horseshoe crabs, and scorpions are all invertebrates. Use the Internet, books, or magazines to research these and other invertebrates. Write a report on one of the invertebrates you read about. Where does it live? What are its habits? Who are its predators? What does it prey on? Include facts and definitions to explain or inform. Organize your report into paragraphs with headings. Share your report.

_____
_____
_____
_____
_____
_____
_____
_____
_____
_____
_____
_____
_____
_____
_____
_____
_____
_____
_____
_____
_____
_____
_____
_____
_____

Name_____

1. The area of the top of a rectangular table is 323 square feet. If the length of the table is 19 feet, what is the width of the table? _____

2. Write the number in word form.

   841,504 _____

3. 75 × 36 = _____

4. Write the equation.
   Grace saw 16 bird habitats at the zoo's aviary. The sign said each habitat had 12 birds. How many birds were in the aviary in all? _____

Everyone seems to like Dan because he is always **amiable**.

1. Circle the word that has its final **e** pronounced.

2. What does **amiable** mean? _____

3. What clues in the sentence gave you the answer to question 2? _____
   _____

4. Does the sentence tell us that everyone likes Dan? _____
   _____

Write a word from the box to complete each definition.

diversity	heredity	inherit	species	trait

1. _____ – the passing of characteristics from one generation to the next

2. _____ – the condition of being different

3. _____ – a group of animals that can reproduce

4. _____ – a feature or characteristic gotten from a parent

5. _____ – to get a characteristic from a parent or ancestor

Supply is the amount of a product that sellers are able to sell. **Demand** is the amount of the product that buyers are willing to buy. A **surplus** of goods is when there is more than enough to satisfy all of the buyers. A **scarcity** of goods is when there isn't enough to go around. When supply and demand are in balance, the price is right for both buyers and sellers.

Draw a line to match each word to its definition.

1. surplus   A. not enough of an item

2. demand   B. what buyers want to buy

3. scarcity   C. what sellers are able to sell

4. supply   D. more than enough of an item

Human beings are all people but have different colors of skin and hair, stand at different heights, and have various talents. The same is true for other species. Why is diversity so important? Write a letter to a science magazine explaining your position. State your opinion clearly and support it with specific reasons and facts. Let your teacher read your rough draft. Make changes if needed. Then, type the letter on a computer.

_____

_____

_____

_____

_____

_____

_____

_____

_____

_____

_____

_____

_____

_____

_____

_____

_____

_____

_____

_____

_____

_____

_____

_____

_____

4.RL.1, 4.RL.4, 4.RL.7, 4.RI.1, 4.RI.4, 4.RF.3, 4.W.1, 4.W.4, 4.W.6, 4.W.10, 4.L.6, 4.OA.A.2, 4.NBT.A.2, 4.NBT.B.5, 4.MD.A.3

Day 1

1. Britney wants to buy 2 shirts that are on sale. Each shirt is on sale for $14, including tax. If Britney has $30, how much change will she get after buying the shirts? _____

2. 30 × 30 = _____

3. 800 ÷ 80 = _____

4. Write **<**, **>**, or **=** to make the statement true.

   136,284 ◯ 134,284

Day 2

Use proofreading marks to correct the capitalization errors.

1. Rosa parks was a brave African american woman who helped make america a better place.

Circle the best phrase to replace the underlined phrase.

2. Everybody knows I <u>didn't mean nothing</u> by it.

   A. did mean nothing   B. didn't mean none   C. didn't mean anything

Add the missing punctuation.

3. Ms Rodriguez showed us a picture of Henry Hudson

Write the correct spelling of the missing word.

4. This _____ (unaforme) is for gym.

Day 3

Write **B** if the adaptation is a behavior. Write **S** if the adaptation is related to structure.

1. _____ thick fur

2. _____ webbed feet

3. _____ flies away for winter

4. _____ builds a nest

5. _____ hisses at unknown animals

6. _____ uses sunlight for energy

Day 4

The production of goods and services depends on three factors. Earth provides natural resources that people use to make things. People's skills at making products or providing services are human resources. The machines, factories, and equipment used to make products or provide services are capital resources.

Read each sentence. Write **T** if it is true. Write **F** if it is false.

1. _____ Labor is needed for production.

2. _____ A dentist needs capital resources to run an office.

3. _____ Workers are human resources.

4. _____ A hammer is an example of a natural resource.

Think about one of your favorite products. It could be a food, a video game, or a pair of shoes. How is it produced? How is it distributed to the seller? What resources are used to produce it? Use the Internet, books, or magazines to find out. Then, write how your favorite product is made and sold. Include facts and definitions to explain. Organize your report into paragraphs with headings.

_____
_____
_____
_____
_____
_____
_____
_____
_____
_____
_____
_____
_____
_____
_____
_____
_____
_____
_____
_____
_____
_____
_____

Name_____

1. Decompose $\frac{3}{5}$ in two ways.

   A. $\frac{1}{5} + \frac{\square}{5} + \frac{\square}{5} = \frac{3}{5}$ B. $\frac{2}{5} + \frac{\square}{5} = \frac{3}{5}$

2. Henry has 342 marbles in bags. If 9 marbles are in each bag, how many bags does Henry have? _____
   How many bags will he have if he gives 15 bags to his brother? _____

Numismatics, or coin collecting, is a very old hobby. It began long ago in other countries. It was not popular right away in America. Most Americans were too busy building a country out of a wilderness to think about collecting coins. It was not until about 1840 that Americans began to become serious coin collectors.

1. Circle all of the words that start with a hard **c**.
2. What is **numismatics**? _____
3. What is the main idea of this paragraph? _____
4. Why did this hobby start so late in America? _____
   _____

1. What is a behavior?
   _____
2. Write a behavior each organism exhibits.

   dog _____

   fish _____

   ant _____

   human _____

In 1869, Thomas Adams was the first to market chewing gum. He got the idea for chewing gum from a Mexican general. General Santa Anna told Adams that he liked to chew a dried tree sap called **chicle**. Thomas thought the chicle was interesting, but it tasted terrible. He decided to add flavoring to it. The idea worked, and he opened a flavored-gum factory where the flavored-gum sold like crazy! In 1871, Thomas **patented** a machine for the manufacture of his gum.

1. What does **patent** mean? _____
2. What is **chicle**? _____
3. Who did Thomas Adams get the idea from for chewing gum?
   _____

Imagine that you could give a gift to anyone in the world. What would the gift be? To whom would you give it? Why would you give this particular gift? What would this person say about the gift? Write a narrative essay. Include details to describe thoughts, feelings, or actions. Include dialogue in your essay. Provide a concluding statement.

_____

_____

_____

_____

_____

_____

_____

_____

_____

_____

_____

_____

_____

_____

_____

_____

_____

_____

_____

_____

_____

_____

_____

 4.RI.1, 4.RI.2, 4.RI.4, 4.RF.3, 4.RF.4, 4.W.3, 4.W.4, 4.W.10, 4.L.6, 4.OA.A.2, 4.NF.B.3

1. 56 × 22 = _____

2. The perimeter of a rectangle is 60 meters. If the length of the rectangle is 14 meters, what is the width of the rectangle? _____

3. If the fraction $\frac{26}{100}$ equals 0.26, then $\frac{33}{100}$ equals _____ .

4. $3\frac{3}{8} + 2\frac{5}{8}$ = _____

In the spring, a horse or donkey may have a foal. It may be a male (a colt) or a female (a filly). The ewes may give birth to lambs at this time too. It is fun to watch the baby animals try to stand while their new legs are still shaky, or wobbly. Near the barn, the goose is careful when tending her goslings, while the family's dog feeds her **whelps**.

1. Circle the word that starts with the same ending sound in **threw**.

2. What is another word for **whelps**? _____

3. As you read this paragraph, where do you imagine it takes place? _____

_____

Unscramble the letters in parentheses to complete each sentence.

1. All living things need _____(greeny) to survive.

2. Plants use light energy to make _____(guras) that they store.

3. An _____(evibrroeh) is an animal that eats plants for energy.

4. A _____(anorvecri) is an animal that eats other animals for energy.

5. An _____(ermovnio) is an animal that gets energy from both plants and animals.

The Aztec people lived in the area that is now central Mexico. The Aztec empire lasted from 1325 to 1521. The Aztecs built temples that were similar to Egyptian pyramids but without the pointed tops. The Aztecs enjoyed many foods, including corn or maize, beans, squash, tomatoes, and chili peppers. The Aztec people are known for their pottery and statues.

1. How long did the Aztec empire last? _____

2. How were their temples different from Egyptian pyramids? _____

_____

3. What are some things the Aztec people are known for?

_____

Write a poem about an experience you have had with an animal. Some examples could be the first time you saw your new puppy, an animal you saw while hiking in the mountains, a groundhog in the backyard, or the fish you caught while deep-sea fishing. Include details to describe thoughts, feelings, or actions. When you have finished writing, read it aloud to someone. Make changes if needed.

_____

_____

_____

_____

_____

_____

_____

_____

_____

_____

_____

_____

_____

_____

_____

_____

_____

_____

_____

_____

_____

_____

4.RL.1, 4.RL.4, 4.RL.7, 4.RI.1, 4.RI.4, 4.RF.3, 4.W.3, 4.W.5, 4.W.8, 4.L.4, 4.L.6, 4.NBT.B.5, 4.NF.B.3, 4.NF.C.6, 4.MD.A.3

CD-104821 • © Carson-Dellosa

1. $13\frac{5}{8} + \frac{7}{8} = $ _____

2. List the factors of 34. _____

    Is this number prime or composite? _____

3. Determine the 13th shape in the pattern. _____ ☆ ▢ ◯

4. If $\frac{6}{10} + \frac{5}{100} = \frac{65}{100}$, then $\frac{5}{10} + \frac{2}{100} = \frac{\square}{100}$.

Use proofreading marks to correct the capitalization errors.

1. Rosa parks was arrested for not giving up her Seat.

Circle the best phrase to replace the underlined phrase.

2. He <u>wouldn't do no work</u>.

    A. wouldn't do any work   B. would not do no work   C. would do any work

Add the missing punctuation.

3. I want to see Baltimore Maryland on the Chesapeake Bay

Write the correct spelling of the word in parenthesis.

4. My new shirt has _____ (daisys) on it.

1. What is an ecosystem?

    _____

2. List three ecosystems.

    _____

3. Choose one ecosystem you listed above and name three living and three nonliving things in it.

    Living: _____

    Nonliving: _____

Landfills are being filled with used toys, dishes, shoes, and other types of plastics. To help **alleviate** this problem, people can recycle. Plastic containers labeled with a recycling symbol can be recycled. Try to reuse containers that cannot be recycled rather than throw them away. Reducing the use of plastic will also help.

1. What does **alleviate** mean? _____

    _____

2. List some things that are made from recycled plastic. _____

    _____

3. How can you reduce the use of plastics in your home? _____

    _____

Think of something that has changed the ecosystem you live in. Consider changes that are human made. Examples might be litter lining the streets, smog, or pollutants in a river. Write a letter to the mayor of your town or city. Describe the effect this change has made on the community. Tell how you feel about it. In the final paragraph of your letter, suggest several ways your town or city can make changes or clean up the area. Include facts and definitions to explain or inform. Use paragraphs to separate topics.

_____

_____

_____

_____

_____

_____

_____

_____

_____

_____

_____

_____

_____

_____

_____

_____

_____

_____

_____

_____

_____

_____

_____

4.RI.1, 4.RF.3, 4.W.2, 4.W.4, 4.L.2, 4.L.3, 4.L.4, 4.OA.B.4, 4.OA.C.5, 4.NF.B.3, 4.NF.C.6

Day 1

1. Write **<**, **>**, or **=** to make the statement true.

    $\frac{5}{10}$ ◯ $\frac{3}{6}$

2. 342 ÷ 6 = _____

3. Write the decimal. $\frac{32}{100}$ = _____

4. The Rossi family ate $\frac{1}{3}$ of a cheese pizza and $\frac{2}{3}$ of a pepperoni pizza.

    How much total pizza did the Rossi family eat? _____

Day 2

This story continues through Week 27.
Speed skater Bonnie Blair is the only American woman to have won five Olympic gold medals.

1. What is Bonnie Blair's specialty? _____

2. What is unique about her? _____

    _____

3. What country did Bonnie represent at the Olympics? _____

Day 3

1. What cycle is shown? Write **1** through **5** to show the order.

    Cycle name: _____

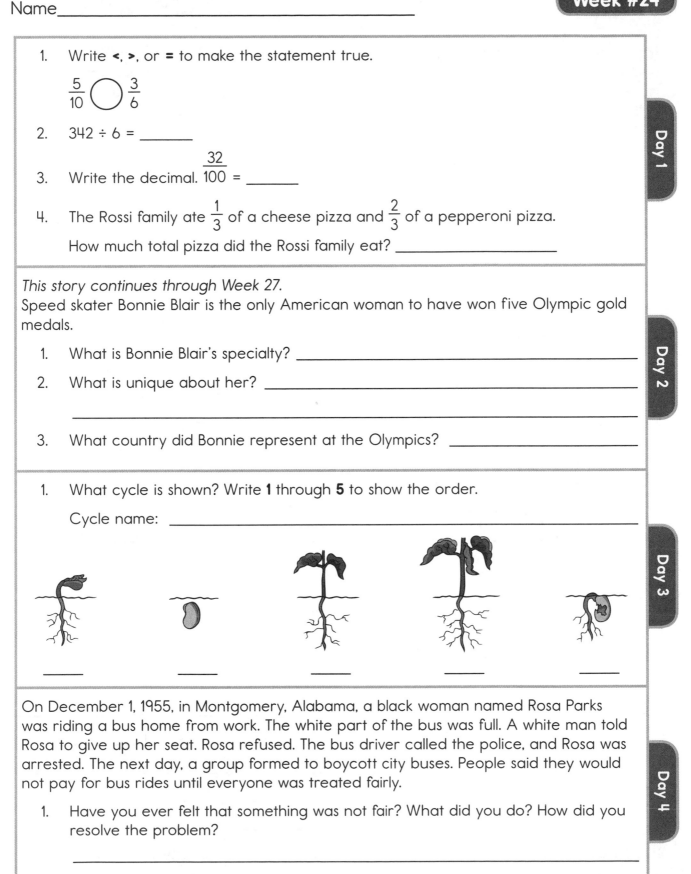

On December 1, 1955, in Montgomery, Alabama, a black woman named Rosa Parks was riding a bus home from work. The white part of the bus was full. A white man told Rosa to give up her seat. Rosa refused. The bus driver called the police, and Rosa was arrested. The next day, a group formed to boycott city buses. People said they would not pay for bus rides until everyone was treated fairly.

Day 4

1. Have you ever felt that something was not fair? What did you do? How did you resolve the problem?

    _____

    _____

Rosa Parks changed life in Montgomery forever with her simple wish to be treated as an equal. Imagine that you were on the same bus as Rosa Parks. You see the argument starting between Rosa and the other man. What could you do or say to prevent the argument and help these two people come to a peaceful solution to the situation? Include dialogue in your narrative. Then, share your writing with a friend. Did they have the same resolution?

_____

_____

_____

_____

_____

_____

_____

_____

_____

_____

_____

_____

_____

_____

_____

_____

_____

_____

_____

_____

_____

_____

_____

4.RI.1, 4.RI.2, 4.RI.3, 4.RI.5, 4.RF.4, 4.W.3, 4.NBT.B.6, 4.NF.A.2, 4.NF.B.3, 4.NF.C.6

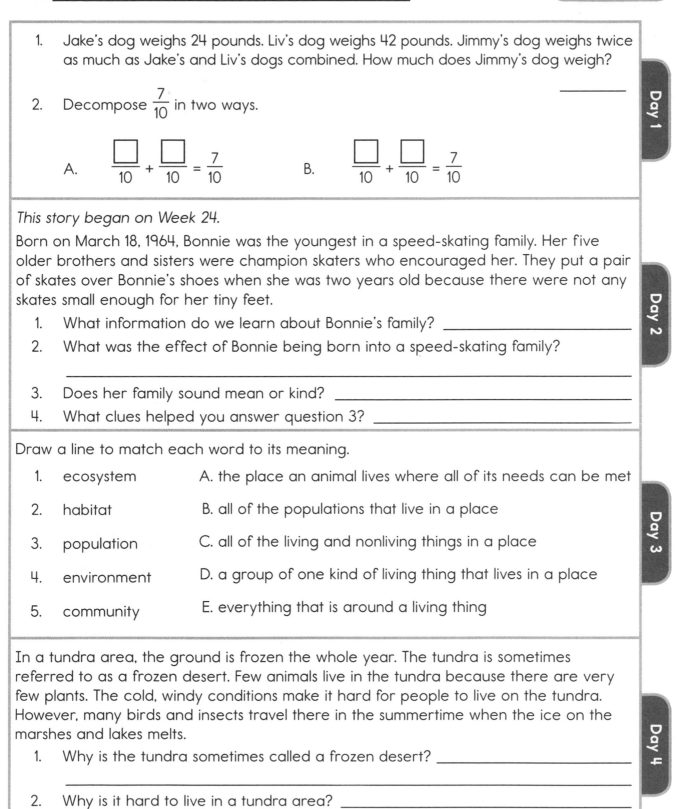

1. Jake's dog weighs 24 pounds. Liv's dog weighs 42 pounds. Jimmy's dog weighs twice as much as Jake's and Liv's dogs combined. How much does Jimmy's dog weigh?

_____

2. Decompose $\frac{7}{10}$ in two ways.

A. $\frac{\square}{10} + \frac{\square}{10} = \frac{7}{10}$ B. $\frac{\square}{10} + \frac{\square}{10} = \frac{7}{10}$

Day 1

This story began on Week 24.

Born on March 18, 1964, Bonnie was the youngest in a speed-skating family. Her five older brothers and sisters were champion skaters who encouraged her. They put a pair of skates over Bonnie's shoes when she was two years old because there were not any skates small enough for her tiny feet.

1. What information do we learn about Bonnie's family? _____

2. What was the effect of Bonnie being born into a speed-skating family?

_____

3. Does her family sound mean or kind? _____

4. What clues helped you answer question 3? _____

Day 2

Draw a line to match each word to its meaning.

1. ecosystem   A. the place an animal lives where all of its needs can be met

2. habitat   B. all of the populations that live in a place

3. population   C. all of the living and nonliving things in a place

4. environment   D. a group of one kind of living thing that lives in a place

5. community   E. everything that is around a living thing

Day 3

In a tundra area, the ground is frozen the whole year. The tundra is sometimes referred to as a frozen desert. Few animals live in the tundra because there are very few plants. The cold, windy conditions make it hard for people to live on the tundra. However, many birds and insects travel there in the summertime when the ice on the marshes and lakes melts.

1. Why is the tundra sometimes called a frozen desert? _____

_____

2. Why is it hard to live in a tundra area? _____

_____

3. Why do you think the birds and insects only travel there in the summer?

_____

Day 4

Name_____

Veterinarians say that there are more overweight pets than ever before. The problem is worse in dogs, but weight problems also occur in cats, rabbits, hamsters, guinea pigs, and birds. Use the Internet, books, or magazines to find out more about this problem and what can be done to help overweight pets. Then, imagine you are a vet. Write a letter to a pet owner that includes a solution to her pet's weight problem. Include facts and definitions to explain or inform. Use paragraphs to separate topics.

_____
_____
_____
_____
_____
_____
_____
_____
_____
_____
_____
_____
_____
_____
_____
_____
_____
_____
_____
_____
_____
_____
_____
_____
_____
_____

4.RI.1, 4.RI.2, 4.RI.3, 4.RI.5, 4.RF.4, 4.W.2, 4.W.4, 4.W.5, 4.W.7, 4.OA.B.3, 4.NF.B.3

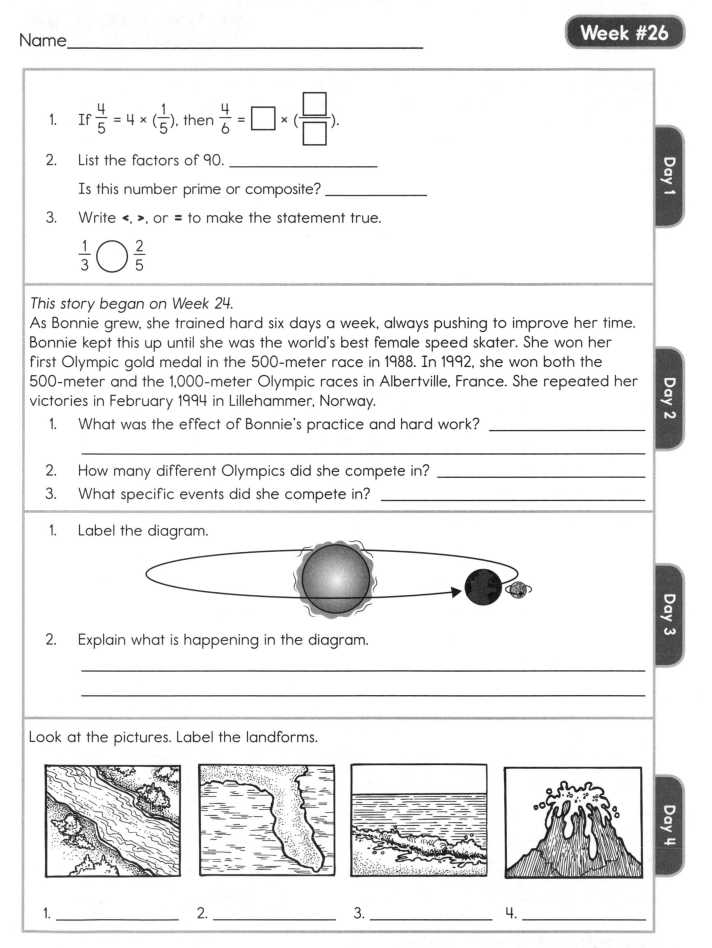

Day 1

1. If $\frac{4}{5} = 4 \times (\frac{1}{5})$, then $\frac{4}{6} = \boxed{} \times (\frac{\boxed{}}{\boxed{}})$.

2. List the factors of 90. _____

   Is this number prime or composite? _____

3. Write **<**, **>**, or **=** to make the statement true.

   $\frac{1}{3}$ ◯ $\frac{2}{5}$

Day 2

This story began on Week 24.
As Bonnie grew, she trained hard six days a week, always pushing to improve her time. Bonnie kept this up until she was the world's best female speed skater. She won her first Olympic gold medal in the 500-meter race in 1988. In 1992, she won both the 500-meter and the 1,000-meter Olympic races in Albertville, France. She repeated her victories in February 1994 in Lillehammer, Norway.

1. What was the effect of Bonnie's practice and hard work? _____

   _____

2. How many different Olympics did she compete in? _____

3. What specific events did she compete in? _____

Day 3

1. Label the diagram.

2. Explain what is happening in the diagram.

   _____

   _____

Day 4

Look at the pictures. Label the landforms.

1. _____   2. _____   3. _____   4. _____

Imagine you are a world-class skier. You are hoping to take home a gold medal at the Winter Olympics. While skiing down a long hill, you take a wrong turn. Write about what you imagine could happen next. Your story can have a realistic or a silly ending. Include details to describe thoughts, feelings, or actions.

_____

_____

_____

_____

_____

_____

_____

_____

_____

_____

_____

_____

_____

_____

_____

_____

_____

_____

_____

_____

_____

_____

_____

_____

_____

_____

_____

_____

1. Write the decimal. $\frac{68}{100}$ = _____

2. $6\frac{3}{5} - 3\frac{1}{5}$ = _____

3. 934×6 = _____

4. Write **<**, **>**, or **=** to make the statement true. 0.46 ◯ 0.32

Day 1

This story began on Week 24.
Bonnie's Olympic successes made her famous all over the world. Bonnie retired from speed skating in 1995 to focus on other competitions.

1. What was the effect of Bonnie's Olympic successes? _____

2. Why did she retire from speed skating? _____

3. Why would someone retire when she is at the top of her game?

_____

4. What information was not in this passage that you would like to know about Bonnie Blair? _____

Day 2

Write **true** or **false**. Rewrite any false statement to make it true.

1. _____ The moon is a satellite that revolves around Earth.

2 _____ It takes exactly 29 days for the moon to circle around Earth.

3. _____ The moon makes its own light.

4. _____ The changes in the moon's shape as seen from Earth are called phases.

Day 3

Almost 2,000 years ago, Pompeii was a rich and beautiful city in the Bay of Naples. The city lay close to a volcano, Mount Vesuvius. The volcano **erupted** and the ash fell so quickly that people were buried wherever they were. Scientists have been studying artifacts from Pompeii for over 200 years.

1. What does **erupt** mean? _____

2. What was the effect of the ash falling so quickly? _____

_____

3. How does the discovery of artifacts help historians? _____

_____

Day 4

Some people think that the full moon is a time when dogs howl and people behave in extraordinary ways. Imagine that whenever there is a full moon, you turn into a person who is exactly the opposite of who you usually are. What does that person look like? How does that person behave? What does that person do on the weekend? Write an essay describing the new you. Use paragraphs to separate topics or complete thoughts. Include details to describe thoughts, feelings, or actions.

_____

_____

_____

_____

_____

_____

_____

_____

_____

_____

_____

_____

_____

_____

_____

_____

_____

_____

_____

_____

_____

_____

_____

_____

_____

Day 1

1. $9 \times \dfrac{3}{4} =$ _____

2. Write the decimal. $\dfrac{4}{10} =$ _____

3. Round 188,206 to the nearest thousand. _____

4. $\dfrac{7}{12} - \dfrac{5}{12} =$ _____

Day 2

"The house looks great!" said Mrs. Bradford. "By the way, we would like to know if you can come back again tomorrow."

"Uh . . . I don't think so, Mrs. Bradford. I'm pretty busy until next year—I mean next week."

While I lay in bed that night, I kept thinking that maybe someone had **reversed** a couple of letters in Bart's name.

1. What two words form the contraction **I'm**? _____

2. What does **reversed** mean? _____

3. What word does the author think Bart's name should be? _____

4. What job do you think the writer has? _____

Day 3

1. What is a mineral?

   _____

2. Write **P** in front of the properties that help scientists classify minerals.

   _____ how hard it is   _____ its color

   _____ how shiny it is   _____ its temperature

   _____ how it breaks   _____ if it is magnetic

   _____ how it smells   _____ its size

Day 4

A **world map** shows the outlines of the continents and seas. A **city map** shows important buildings and streets. Maps use symbols. A **legend** explains the symbols used on a map. A **scale** tells how distances on the map relate to actual distances.
Draw a line to match each word to its definition.

1. legend   A. shows outline of continents and seas

2. world map   B. gives you the distance related to real world

3. scale   C. shows important buildings and streets

4. city map   D. explains the symbols on a map

Look at a world map or globe. Choose a country that you would like to travel to. Use books, magazines, or the Internet to find out more about it. What is the capital? What is the best way to travel there? Research the climate in that area. Describe the culture or cultures of that country. Write an informative essay. Include facts and definitions to inform. Organize your essay with headings. Share your report with a classmate.

_____

_____

_____

_____

_____

_____

_____

_____

_____

_____

_____

_____

_____

_____

_____

_____

_____

_____

_____

_____

_____

_____

_____

Day 1

1. Sixty-five campers arrive. Nine go home early. If 8 people sleep in 1 tent, how many tents will the campers need? _____

2. Kim needs $\frac{2}{4}$ of a gallon of water for her balloon. Seth needs $\frac{3}{4}$ of a gallon of water for his balloon. How much more water does Seth need than Kim? _____

3. Write the decimal.

   $\frac{28}{100}$ = _____

Day 2

Dear Raul,

   Hey, I miss you! It is so quiet here at my grandmother's house. She doesn't own a TV! She must be the last person on the planet without one. All morning long, we sit and read. Next, we eat lunch and then go for a little walk. After that, we read some more. The only time I get to see anyone is when we shop for groceries.

1. What is Raul's problem? _____

2. What is the first thing the author says in this letter? _____

3. Can you imagine spending the summer without TV? _____

4. Do you think the author looks forward to going out for groceries? _____

Day 3

1. Identify two reasons that scientists study fossils.

   _____

   _____

2. How can knowing about organisms living today help scientists understand about life long ago?

   _____

   _____

   _____

Day 4

A **physical map** shows geographic features of the land. A **climate map** gives information about the climate and precipitation in an area. A **road map** shows major highways and roads. An **economic map** shows the type of natural or economic resources in an area. Draw a line to match each map to its use.

1. climate map   A. to determine the terrain on a hiking trip

2. road map   B. to plan a trip into the city

3. physical map   C. to find out which state produces the most corn

4. economic map   D. yearly rainfall totals in an area

The fourth week of June is National Camping Week in the United States. Plan a camping trip for your family. Make a list of everything you would need to take along. You should consider personal care items such as toothbrushes and extra clothing. Also, think about what you want to do. Will you need fishing gear or hiking poles? How about cooking utensils? There is a lot to think about. Make sure your essay includes as much as you can think of. Then, read it to someone who has already been camping. Make changes as needed.

_____

_____

_____

_____

_____

_____

_____

_____

_____

_____

_____

_____

_____

_____

_____

_____

_____

_____

_____

_____

_____

_____

_____

_____

 4.RL.1, 4.RI.2, 4.RF.4, 4.W.2, 4.W.5, 4.OA.B.3, 4.NF.B.4, 4.NF.C.6

CD-104821 • © Carson-Dellosa

1. $\dfrac{\square}{10} = \dfrac{30}{100}$

2. The candy jar has 251 pieces of candy. Roxanne adds 31 pieces of candy to it. If the candy is divided equally between 6 campers, how many pieces will each camper get? _____

3. If $\dfrac{4}{5} = 4 \times (\dfrac{1}{5})$, then $\dfrac{6}{6} = \square \times (\dfrac{\square}{\square})$.

Would you eat bugs? Many people know that bugs taste good and are good for you. In other parts of the world, eating insects is not unusual. Some insects have high nutritional value. Dried insects are 60 to 70 percent protein. Some insects are rich in lysine, an amino acid that helps muscles develop.

1. What words have a soft **c** sound in the middle? _____

2. What other words could you use instead of "good" and "good for you" in the second sentence? _____

3. What percentage of dried insects contain protein? _____

4. Did the writer of this paragraph write it to convince you to eat a bug today or to inform you about bugs being healthy to eat? _____

Circle the word that best completes each sentence.

1. (Weathering, Deposition) is the settling of rocks and soil following erosion.

2. The eroded materials fall out once the water or wind (quickens, slows).

3. The soil in these areas is filled with rich (nutrients, gases) that are good for crops.

4. Depositions caused by wind can form (mountains, dunes).

5. Depositions caused by ocean water can form new (bays, beaches).

6. In a river, deposition can create a (delta, canyon).

1. At what degree north can you find the North Pole? _____

2. What is the 0° latitude line called? _____

3. The portion of the globe from 0° latitude to the South Pole is the _____ hemisphere.

Ant eggs cooked in butter are commonly eaten in Mexico. People in Bolivia munch on roasted ants as if they were peanuts. Crickets, caterpillars, termites, bees, and wasps also show up on menus around the world. Would you eat bugs? Write an essay expressing your opinion in the first paragraph or two. Then, think about what you would do if you had no other food. What insects might you consider eating? Would you pop them in your mouth raw, or would you cook them? Give reasons to support your opinions.

_____
_____
_____
_____
_____
_____
_____
_____
_____
_____
_____
_____
_____
_____
_____
_____
_____
_____
_____
_____
_____
_____
_____
_____

Day 1

1. Complete the table.

2. Draw an example of parallel lines.

3. 3,766 ÷ 7 = _____

m	cm
1	100
2	
3	
4	
5	
6	
7	

Day 2

Use proofreading marks to correct the capitalization errors.

1. the north American grizzly bear is rare in the United states.

Underline the correct form of the present-tense verb.

2. Every day I (jog, jogs) in the park.

Add the correct punctuation to the quotation.

3. Benjamin Franklin said Early to bed and early to rise makes a man healthy wealthy and wise

Combine the words with the suffixes to make abstract nouns.

4. citizen + -ship = _____   imagine + -ation = _____

Day 3

1. What causes an earthquake?

   _____

   _____

2. How does an earthquake change the land? Give two examples.

   _____

   _____

   _____

Day 4

1. What is the line at 0° longitude called? _____

2. From the Prime Meridian east to 180° longitude is called the _____ hemisphere.

3. From the Prime Meridian west to 180° longitude is called the _____ hemisphere.

When an earthquake hits, there is little time to think. Most people immediately rush outside or duck under something. Sometimes earthquakes are destructive. People lose homes or other things of great value. If you were in an earthquake and could only grab one object on your way to safety, what would it be? Write an essay about it. Describe it and tell why the object is important to you. Include details to describe your thoughts, feelings, or actions. Share your essay with another classmate. Make changes if necessary.

_____

_____

_____

_____

_____

_____

_____

_____

_____

_____

_____

_____

_____

_____

_____

_____

_____

_____

_____

_____

_____

_____

_____

_____

4.RF.3, 4.W.3, 4.W.5, 4.L.1, 4.L.2, 4.L.4, 4.L.6, 4.NBT.B.6, 4.MD.A.1, 4.G.A.1

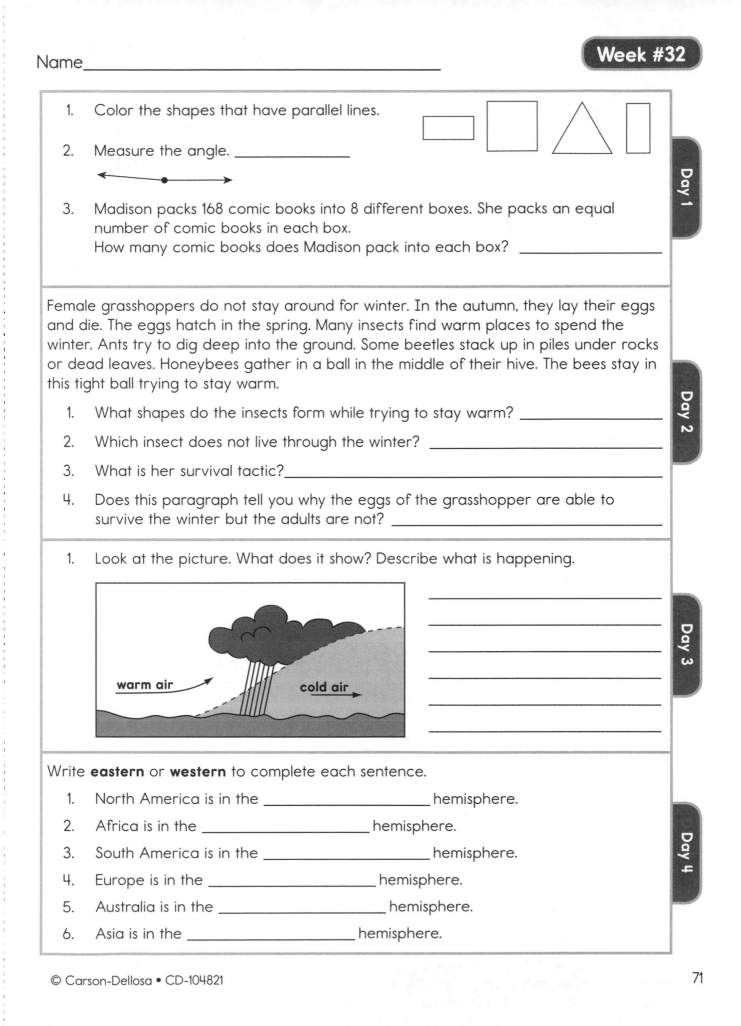

1. Color the shapes that have parallel lines.

2. Measure the angle. _____

3. Madison packs 168 comic books into 8 different boxes. She packs an equal number of comic books in each box.
How many comic books does Madison pack into each box? _____

Day 1

Female grasshoppers do not stay around for winter. In the autumn, they lay their eggs and die. The eggs hatch in the spring. Many insects find warm places to spend the winter. Ants try to dig deep into the ground. Some beetles stack up in piles under rocks or dead leaves. Honeybees gather in a ball in the middle of their hive. The bees stay in this tight ball trying to stay warm.

1. What shapes do the insects form while trying to stay warm? _____

2. Which insect does not live through the winter? _____

3. What is her survival tactic?_____

4. Does this paragraph tell you why the eggs of the grasshopper are able to survive the winter but the adults are not? _____

Day 2

1. Look at the picture. What does it show? Describe what is happening.

warm air   cold air

_____
_____
_____
_____
_____
_____

Day 3

Write **eastern** or **western** to complete each sentence.

1. North America is in the _____ hemisphere.

2. Africa is in the _____ hemisphere.

3. South America is in the _____ hemisphere.

4. Europe is in the _____ hemisphere.

5. Australia is in the _____ hemisphere.

6. Asia is in the _____ hemisphere.

Day 4

Name_____

Look at a world map or globe. Choose a continent. What types of animals live on that continent? Use the Internet, books, or magazines to find out. Then, write a report about the kinds of animals and their habitats in that part of the world. Include facts and definitions to inform. Use headings and illustrations to organize your report. Type your report on a computer. Share your report with a classmate.

_____
_____
_____
_____
_____
_____
_____
_____
_____
_____
_____
_____
_____
_____
_____
_____
_____
_____
_____
_____
_____
_____
_____
_____
_____

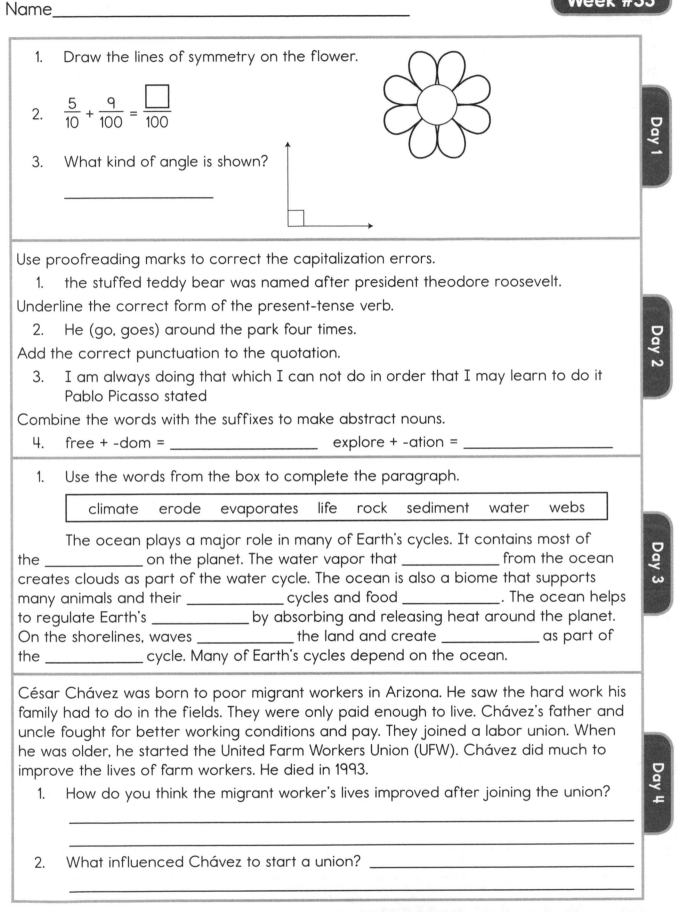

Day 1

1. Draw the lines of symmetry on the flower.

2. $\dfrac{5}{10} + \dfrac{9}{100} = \dfrac{\boxed{}}{100}$

3. What kind of angle is shown?

   _____

Day 2

Use proofreading marks to correct the capitalization errors.

1. the stuffed teddy bear was named after president theodore roosevelt.

Underline the correct form of the present-tense verb.

2. He (go, goes) around the park four times.

Add the correct punctuation to the quotation.

3. I am always doing that which I can not do in order that I may learn to do it Pablo Picasso stated

Combine the words with the suffixes to make abstract nouns.

4. free + -dom = _____   explore + -ation = _____

Day 3

1. Use the words from the box to complete the paragraph.

   | climate   erode   evaporates   life   rock   sediment   water   webs |

       The ocean plays a major role in many of Earth's cycles. It contains most of the _____ on the planet. The water vapor that _____ from the ocean creates clouds as part of the water cycle. The ocean is also a biome that supports many animals and their _____ cycles and food _____. The ocean helps to regulate Earth's _____ by absorbing and releasing heat around the planet. On the shorelines, waves _____ the land and create _____ as part of the _____ cycle. Many of Earth's cycles depend on the ocean.

Day 4

César Chávez was born to poor migrant workers in Arizona. He saw the hard work his family had to do in the fields. They were only paid enough to live. Chávez's father and uncle fought for better working conditions and pay. They joined a labor union. When he was older, he started the United Farm Workers Union (UFW). Chávez did much to improve the lives of farm workers. He died in 1993.

1. How do you think the migrant worker's lives improved after joining the union?

   _____

   _____

2. What influenced Chávez to start a union? _____

   _____

Take a piece of paper and fold it horizontally and vertically, one time each way. Cut shapes and lines from the unfolded edges. Open the paper and you will see a perfectly symmetrical shape. What animal does it remind you of? Add features and body parts with a pen, pencil, or markers. Then write about your creature, imaginary or real. Describe where the animal lives and how it meets its basic needs. If it is an imaginary creature, make up a name for it. Use paragraphs to organize your story.

_____

_____

_____

_____

_____

_____

_____

_____

_____

_____

_____

_____

_____

_____

_____

_____

_____

_____

_____

_____

_____

_____

_____

_____

Day 1

1. Measure the angle.

   _____

2. Write the equation.

   Maria is 8 years old. Her mom is 4 times as old as Maria is. How old is Maria's mom?

   _____

3. Nikki's Italian Restaurant put $\frac{1}{4}$ of a gallon of oil in one batch of salad dressing.

   How many gallons of oil would be used in 4 batches of salad dressing? _____

Day 2

Salvador Dali painted in an unusual style. The items you see in Dali's works are things you might see every day, but Dali changed them. He made them look unusual. For example, one of his paintings shows clocks that are melting.

1. **Un-** is a prefix that means "not." What does **unusual** mean? _____
2. What other words could you use instead of **unusual**? _____
3. What detail tells you about Dali's painting style? _____
4. Why did the writer write the paragraph?

   A. to entertain   B. to inform   C. to give an opinion

Day 3

1. What is technology?

   _____

   _____

2. List four ways you use technology each day.

   _____

   _____

   _____

Day 4

Gaylord Nelson, a US senator, was trying to come up with ideas that would reunite the nation during the Vietnam War. April 22 was chosen as the day to celebrate Earth Day by Congress. Packets and kits with ideas and suggestions to celebrate were mailed to schools all over the US. Over 20 million Americans participated in activities all across the nation. Earth Day is still celebrated today on April 22nd.

1. Draw a colorful bumper sticker that would tell people about Earth Day and what it represents.

Name_____

Imagine that you are the art critic for a large city newspaper. Use the Internet or books to choose an artwork and a critique. Then, write a news story about it as if it had just been painted. Include the name of the painting and the artist's name. Include facts and definitions to explain and inform. Since you are a critic, your opinion of the artwork is also important. Give reasons to support your opinion. Include a copy of the artwork to illustrate your critique.

_____

_____

_____

_____

_____

_____

_____

_____

_____

_____

_____

_____

_____

_____

_____

_____

_____

_____

_____

_____

_____

_____

_____

_____

Name_____

Day 1

1. What is the measure of the complete angle? _____

2. Zoe was collecting marbles. She got 10 marbles from the store and 5 from her mom. Zoe's teacher gave her 18 marbles. Zoe gave 12 marbles to her friend Xia. How many marbles does Zoe have left? _____

3. 985 ÷ 8 = _____

4. Jasper needs 180 inches of string for his project. How many yards should he buy? _____

Day 2

The spaceship had been traveling through space for 200 years. The people on board were just coming out of **stasis**. They had not been awake since 2020. The computer was set to wake them when the planet X59 was a week's travel away.

1. Circle the compound word in the passage.

2. What does it mean to be in **stasis**? _____

3. What clues from the paragraph helped you answer question 2? _____

_____

4. How far away is planet X59? _____

Day 3

Engineers use research, science, technology, math, and creativity to create solutions to everyday problems. They design and build things that can be useful in many areas of life. Like scientists, engineers follow a process. They start with a problem they would like to solve. Then, they research, brainstorm, plan, and create a sample. They test and improve their design. Sometimes, they start over! Engineers help improve our daily lives.

1. How are engineers and scientists the same? How are they different? Underline the text in the passage that helped you answer. _____

_____

_____

Day 4

Symbols represent ideas or things. A symbol can represent your favorite sports team or your school. A flag can be a symbol for a country. Symbols in buildings help you know which restroom to use. They can also designate areas in buildings that are accessible to people who use wheelchairs.

1. Where are other places you have seen symbols? _____

2. Draw a symbol that represents you or your family.

Engineers use their products to solve problems. Think of a problem you would like to solve. Design an invention for it. Write a description of the invention, the name, and explain how it solves the problem. Use paragraphs to separate topics. Then, create a brochure to market your invention. Be sure to include a price. Include facts and definitions to explain or inform.

_____

_____

_____

_____

_____

_____

_____

_____

_____

_____

_____

_____

_____

_____

_____

_____

_____

_____

_____

_____

_____

_____

_____

_____

_____

4.RI.1, 4.RI.4, 4.RI.10, 4.RF.4, 4.W.2, 4.W.4, 4.L.4, 4.OA.B.3, 4.NBT.B.6, 4.MD.C.6

1. What is the measure of the complete angle?

   _____

   51°

   12°

2. Is every square a quadrilateral?
   Why or why not? _____

3. Write the decimal.

   $\frac{56}{100} =$ _____

Day 1

Mold is a kind of plant called a fungus. The most common molds are green or black. Mold likes to grow in moist, warm places. But, where does it come from? Mold comes from spores, which exist in the air. If these spores find a moist, warm place, they will produce mold. Mold grows in webs of fuzzy branches. It continues to grow as long as the conditions are right.

1. What is **mold**? _____

2. Where does mold come from? _____

3. Where does mold like to grow? _____

4. What image does the author use to describe how mold grows? _____
   _____

Day 2

Write three foods that belong in each food group.

1. Grains: _____

2. Vegetables: _____

3. Fruits: _____

4. Dairy: _____

5. Proteins: _____

6. Oils: _____

Day 3

There is a certain etiquette that shows proper respect and treatment of a country's flag. For example, the US flag can only be flown upside down as a distress signal. The flag is flown at half-staff when there is a period of national mourning. When the flag is lowered, no part of it should touch the ground or any other object. The US flag is flown above any other flag on the same pole.

1. When can the US flag be flown upside down? _____
   _____

2. When is the flag flown at half-staff? _____

3. Why is it important to show respect for a country's flag? _____
   _____

Day 4

Name_____

Use the Internet, books, or magazines to find out more about the US flag. Then, write a report about the origin of the flag. Include facts and definitions to explain or inform. Organize your report with paragraphs and headings. Show your teacher. Make changes as needed.

_____

_____

_____

_____

_____

_____

_____

_____

_____

_____

_____

_____

_____

_____

_____

_____

_____

_____

_____

_____

_____

_____

_____

4.RI.1, 4.RI.2, 4.RI.7, 4.RF.4, 4.W.2, 4.W.7, 4.L.4, 4.NF.C.6, 4.MD.C.6, 4.G.A.2

1. What is the value of the missing angle?

   _____

   ? 89° 127°

2. List the factors of 87. _____
   Is this number prime or composite? _____

3. Mrs. Lopez wanted to give 20 students calculators. Each calculator weighed 16 ounces. If Mrs. Lopez gave each student a calculator, how many pounds did the calculators weigh in all? _____

Day 1

Use proofreading marks to correct the capitalization errors.

1. Today, my class saw an exhibit in denver called "remember the Children: Daniel's Story."

Write the correct pronoun to complete the sentence.

2. _____ (I, me) have always wanted to go snorkeling.

Fill in the circle by the words and punctuation that correctly complete the sentence.

3. Daniel had two _____ of bread and a sack of _____ for lunch _____ loves food.
   O loafs   O potatoies   O . He
   O loafes   O potatos   O ; he
   O loaves   O potatoes   O , He

Day 2

Write a word to correctly complete each sentence.

1. Adding harmful materials to the environment causes _____.

2. Dumping trash on the ground results in _____ pollution.

3. Construction sites using heavy equipment and loud music produce _____ pollution.

4. Sewage and oil leaking into ponds, lakes, streams, and oceans make _____ pollution.

5. _____ pollution is a big problem because it can affect our breathing and the temperature balance on Earth.

Day 3

The Statue of Liberty was a gift meant to celebrate the spirit of liberty and the friendship of France with the United States. Over the years, it has also become a symbol of freedom and opportunity that the United States offers. Draw a line to match each feature of the Statue of Liberty to its meaning.

1. broken chain at her feet   A. the light of liberty

2. crown with seven spikes   B. breaking free from tyranny

3. shining torch   C. seven seas and continents

4. flowing robe   D. the Roman goddess of liberty

Day 4

Invent an imaginary math monster. What does it look like? How does it help you solve math problems? Can it help students with their homework? Write an essay about your imaginary math monster. Give it a name. Include details to describe thoughts, feelings, or actions. Provide a concluding statement. Share your essay with a classmate.

_____

_____

_____

_____

_____

_____

_____

_____

_____

_____

_____

_____

_____

_____

_____

_____

_____

_____

_____

_____

_____

_____

4.W.3, 4.W.4, 4.L.1, 4.L.2, 4.L.3, 4.L.4, 4.L.6, 4.OA.B.4, 4.MD.A.2, 4.MD.C.7

Day 1

1. $4,893 \div 3 =$ _____

2. Write **<**, **>**, or **=** to make the statement true.

   $\frac{1}{8}$ $\bigcirc$ $\frac{1}{4}$

3. $7\frac{5}{8} - 6\frac{3}{8} =$ _____

4. 4 kilometers = _____ centimeters

Day 2

A mermaid is a creature whose head and upper body are a beautiful woman. The lower body is a fish. Mermaids tend to fall in love with humans. They may try to lure sailors into the ocean with them.

1. Does the **ea** in **creatures** sound like the **ea** in **create** or **features**? _____

2. Does **lure** mean **attract** or **warn**? _____

3. Circle the words that tell us whether mermaids always do the things in this paragraph.

4. Does a mermaid sound like a real or an imaginary creature? _____
   _____

Day 3

1. What does the picture show?
   _____
   _____
   _____
   _____

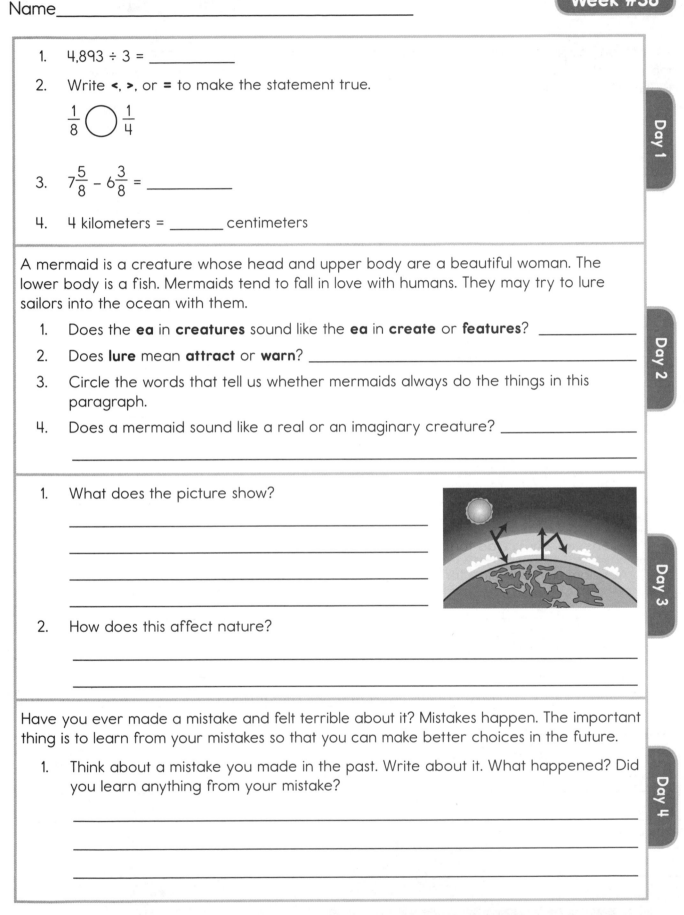

2. How does this affect nature?
   _____
   _____

Day 4

Have you ever made a mistake and felt terrible about it? Mistakes happen. The important thing is to learn from your mistakes so that you can make better choices in the future.

1. Think about a mistake you made in the past. Write about it. What happened? Did you learn anything from your mistake?
   _____
   _____
   _____

Write an imaginary story about finding a mermaid at the beach. Describe the mermaid and the setting. Include dialogue. What would you say to a mermaid? How would she answer? Include details to describe thoughts, feelings, or actions.

_____

_____

_____

_____

_____

_____

_____

_____

_____

_____

_____

_____

_____

_____

_____

_____

_____

_____

_____

_____

_____

_____

_____

_____

_____

_____

_____

Name_____

Week #39

Day 1

Day 2

Day 3

Day 4

Use the line plot to answer the questions.

1. What is the difference between the longest distance run and the shortest distance run?

_____

Miles Run

2. If you added all of the distances together, what would be the total distance run?

_____

$$8 \quad 8\frac{1}{4} \quad 8\frac{2}{4} \quad 8\frac{3}{4} \quad 9 \quad 9\frac{1}{4} \quad 9\frac{2}{4} \quad 9\frac{3}{4} \quad 10$$

George Washington Carver was a scientist. He discovered more than 300 uses for the peanut plant. Among his discoveries were shampoo, car grease, soap, rubber, wood filler, paint, and shoe polish. His research helped farmers.

1. What was the effect of George's research? _____

2. What character traits did George have? _____

3. Do you agree that George Washington Carver is incredible? Why or why not?

_____

_____

---

1. What is a natural resource?

_____

_____

2. Write **R** beside each item that is a natural resource.

_____ air   _____ corn   _____ water

_____ cow   _____ rock   _____ coal

_____ shirt   _____ electricity   _____ paper

When you have a problem, it can be helpful to ask others for advice. Being prepared and knowing what to do in certain situations can help you make good choices.

1. Think about each situation. Circle one and write an appropriate solution to the problem. Share your solution with a classmate.

   A. Another student is bullying you at recess.

   B. A classmate asks you for answers on a test.

_____

_____

_____

Name_____

Nonrenewable resources are natural resources that cannot be replaced. Once they have been used, they are gone forever. Use the Internet or books to find out more about nonrenewable resources. Choose one. Write about how life on earth would change if it disappeared forever. Include facts and definitions to explain or inform. Use paragraphs to separate topics.

_____

_____

_____

_____

_____

_____

_____

_____

_____

_____

_____

_____

_____

_____

_____

_____

_____

_____

_____

_____

_____

_____

_____

4.RI.1, 4.RI.2, 4.RI.5, 4.RF.4, 4.W.2, 4.W.4, 4.W.6, 4.MD.B.4   CD-104821 • © Carson-Dellosa

Name_____

1. 7 hours = _____ seconds

2. A cafeteria has 23 tables. If 15 students can sit at each table, how many students can eat in the cafeteria at the same time? _____

3. $\frac{8}{12} - \frac{7}{12} =$ _____

4. Circle the words that describe the shape.

    trapezoid   rhombus   quadrilateral   rectangle

Use proofreading marks to correct the capitalization errors.

1. one display showed how the nazi Party made unfair rules for jewish people.

Write the correct pronoun to complete the sentence.

2. _____ (He, Him) has been snorkeling for many years.

Fill in the circle by the words and punctuation that correctly complete the sentence.

3. Ten _____ sat on the _____ of the tree _____ were looking at me!

    ○ monkieys   ○ branchs   ○ ; they

    ○ monkeys   ○ branches   ○ . They

    ○ monkeyes   ○ branchies   ○ . they

Unscramble the letters in parentheses to complete each sentence.

1. People practice _____(rasvencoonit) when they protect and use natural resources wisely.

2. Some animal populations, like the dinosaurs, are _____(cixtent).

3. Other populations are _____(gadneenerd), meaning there are few of them left.

4. Many people work together to _____(torcept) these organisms.

5. They put aside land as a _____(furege) where the plants and animals can live in safety.

A time line organizes events by the order in which they occurred. It can be a useful tool for organizing and studying information about a person's life or a historical event.

1. Create a time line of your life. Start with the date of your birth. Place important events that you have experienced, with the date they occurred, on the time line.

    _____

Think about this past school year. Create a time line on the blank line below. Include important events like field trips, special assemblies or speakers, and class projects. Then, choose one event from the time line and write about it. Include details to describe thoughts, feelings, and actions. Provide a conclusion. Share your writing with a classmate.

_____

_____

_____

_____

_____

_____

_____

_____

_____

_____

_____

_____

_____

_____

_____

_____

_____

_____

4.W.3, 4.L.1, 4.L.2, 4.L.3, 4.L.4, 4.L.6, 4.OA.A.2, 4.NF.B.3, 4.MD.A.1, 4.G.A.2

Page 9
Day 1: 1. 65,303; 2. 20 students; 3. 10;
Day 2: 1. knees, kneepads; 2. fell, bumped;
3. he fell; 4. His hands were badly scraped.
Day 3: 1. ruler; 2. thermometer; 3. balance
scale; 4. graduated cylinder; 5. clock or
stopwatch; **Day 4:** 1. Answers will vary.

Page 10
Answers will vary but should be divided into at
least two paragraphs.

Page 11
Day 1: 1. 67,134; 2. 96 cents; 3. pentagon;
4. 50,000; **Day 2:** 1. (first letters of the following
words underlined) rose, parade, new, year's,
eve; 2. am; 3. ?; 4. teeth, women, mice;
Day 3: 1. the metric system; 2. The metric
system allows scientists around the world to
understand the data gathered and repeat
experiments, even if they do not speak the
same language. **Day 4:** 1. Answers will vary but
may include that it is customary for teachers
to have control of their classroom and enforce
the rules. 2. Answers will vary but may include
that government, state, and local laws give
police officers authority to write tickets to
citizens who break laws.

Page 12
Answers will vary but should be divided into
at least two paragraphs and include details to
describe thoughts, feelings, or actions.

Page 13
Day 1: 1. >; 2. 100, 120, 140; 3. 110; 4. 1, 2, 3, 4, 6,
12; composite; **Day 2:** 1. developed, serious,
magnitude (three times), area; 2. the size or
seriousness of an earthquake; 3. People can
feel the earthquake, but it does little damage.
4. The earthquake is more serious. It does
more damage. **Day 3:** 1. B; 2. A; 3. E; 4. F; 5. D;
6. C; **Day 4:** 1. F; 2. F; 3. T; 4. T; 5. T

Page 14
Answers will vary but should contain the
proper steps to conducting a science
experiment and include each of the science
process skills. Allow time for revision.

Page 15
Day 1: 1. 363; 2. 3 × 5 = 15; 3. 60, 90, 120;
4. 1, 11; prime; **Day 2:** 1. (first letter of the
following words underlined) arbor, day; 2. are;
3. ?; 4. oxen, moose, fish; **Day 3:** 1. true; 2. false;
3. false; 4. false; 5. true; **Day 4:** 1–3. Answers
will vary.

Page 16
Answers will vary.

Page 17
Day 1: 1. 32,422; 2. <; 3. 8, 4, 4; 4. The 18th shape is
a circle. **Day 2:** 1. the Underground Railroad and
a train; 2. The Underground Railroad and a train
move people along routes. 3. The underground
tunnels were dirt with no tracks. 4. Answers
will vary. **Day 3:** 1. Answers will vary.
Day 4: 1. Primary sources are diary, original
art, and letters. Secondary sources are
encyclopedia, newspaper, and textbook.

Page 18
Answers will vary but should include details to
describe thoughts, feelings, or actions.

Answer Key

Page 19

Day 1: 1. 7,700; 2. Check students' answers; 3. $14; 4. $222; **Day 2:** 1. (circled) eating, green, green, eat, peas, key; 2. said, called, yelled, pronounced; 3. He will be surprised and disappointed and will want to change his mind. 4. He wanted to get out of eating peas and broccoli. **Day 3:** 1. O; 2. I; 3. O; 4. O; 5. I; **Day 4:** 1. Answers will vary but may include mayor, police chief or city council members. 2. They make the rules for the city. 3. Answers will vary but may include volunteer in the community.

Page 20

Answers will vary but should include prewriting, research, and follow-up.

Page 21

Day 1: 1. 585, 575, 565; 2. $7\frac{1}{4}$ inches; 3. >; **Day 2:** 1. let us, it is; 2. Answers will vary but may include speed, run, go fast, or zoom. 3. B; 4. Answers will vary but may include hamsters don't like to stay in their cages. **Day 3:** 1. Matter is anything that has mass and occupies space. 2. Answers will vary but may include an orange is a solid on the outside, has some liquid on the inside, is round, or is orange in color. **Day 4:** 1. Answers will vary but may include the government pays city park employees to clean the parks and plant flowers. 2. Answers will vary.

Page 22

Answers will vary. Allow time for revision.

Page 23

Day 1: 1. 1, 2, 7, 14; composite; 2. <, <, >; 3. 154, 157, 160; **Day 2:** 1. (first letter of the following words underlined) new, york, pennsylvania; 2. Their; 3. (commas placed after) Iroquois, Ojibwa, Lakota; 4. stopped, wagged, hummed; **Day 3:** 1. P; 2. C; 3. P; 4. C; 5. P; 6. C; 7. P; 8. P; 9. C; 10. P; **Day 4:** 1. A; 2. A

Page 24

Answers will vary but should include details to describe, thoughts, feelings, or actions.

Page 25

Day 1: 1. 95,175; 2. 8 golf clubs; 3. 5 × 5 = 25, 25 × 4 = 100; 4. $13,852; **Day 2:** 1. near the Congress Avenue Bridge; 2. There is a cloud of bats coming from under the bridge. 3. amazed; 4. yes, sundown; **Day 3:** 1. C; 2. E; 3. A; 4. D; 5. F; 6. B; **Day 4:** 1. Answers will vary.

Page 26

Answers will vary but should include four paragraphs, each stating a separate reason.

Page 27

Day 1: 1. 1, 2, 4, 5, 10, 20; composite; 2. 20 cm; 3. yes; 4. 10; **Day 2:** 1. (first letter of the following words underlined) cheyenne, wyoming; (lowercase strike through the first letter) Tribe; 2. There; 3. (comma placed after) Aberdeen; 4. tried, hurried, studied; **Day 3:** 1. Energy changes from electrical to radiant. 2. Energy changes from chemical to mechanical and thermal. **Day 4:** 1. B; 2. C; 3. A; 4. D; 5. Answers will vary.

Page 28

Answers will vary but should be based on research and accompanied with an illustration.

Page 29
Day 1: 1. 21 tourists; 2. 1, 79; prime; 3. 65,932; 4. 70 square meters; **Day 2:** 1. wouldn't; 2. tough, will not give up; 3. To tell us about Crazy Horse. 4. To keep the Native American way of life from disappearing. **Day 3:** 1. gravity; 2. friction; 3. inertia; 4. The force of gravity is helping to pull a person down the stairs. A person walking up the stairs is going against the force of gravity, so it will be a harder task.
Day 4: 1. Check students' drawings.

Page 30
Answers will vary but should show understanding based on research. Allow time for revision.

Page 31
Day 1: 1. 21 inches; 2. 69,600; 3. 439,000; 4. 246; **Day 2:** 1. to do too much; 2. (circled) "Do schoolwork, but take it easy."; 3. two; 4. Answers will vary. **Day 3:** 1. battery or energy source; 2. wire; 3. switch; 4. bulb; 5. The diagram shows a closed circuit. **Day 4:** 1. Answers will vary but may include the ship is powered by an engine and the food is fresh.

Page 32
Answers will vary but should include details to describe thoughts, feelings, or actions.

Page 33
Day 1: 1. 928; 2. 265,276; 3. 17,433; 4. 7 × 9 = 63; **Day 2:** 1. (circled) theropods, resources, dinosaur, decided, another; 2. places to find information; 3. No, because it is hard to find information about them. 4. They will look for information everywhere. **Day 3:** 1. poles; 2. south; 3. north; 4. attract; 5. repel; **Day 4:** 1. B; 2. D; 3. C; 4. A; 5. Answers will vary.

Page 34
Answers will vary but should include information found by polling classmates.

Page 35
Day 1: 1. 294; 2. 34,989; 3. 10; 4. 2 feet; **Day 2:** 1. tarantula; 2. small, tiny, little; bald, smooth; 3. C; 4. You might bother a sleeping tarantula, or a tarantula might bite you.
Day 3: 1. door locks; 2. hard drives; 3. generators; 4. cranes; **Day 4:** 1. He was getting old and felt the water would make him young forever. 2. Florida

Page 36
Answers will vary but should reflect thought, research, and revision. Look for reasons to support the student's opinion. Allow time for interaction with a classmate.

Page 37
Day 1: 1. 44,335; 2. 5,892; 3. 1, 2, 4, 17, 34, 68; composite; 4. 12 inches; **Day 2:** 1. (circled) catch; 2. A; 3. Its poison cannot kill humans. 4. The poison in its bite. **Day 3:** 1. Students should circle the sound wave with crests and troughs that are farther apart. 2. Answers will vary but may include the vibration in something with a low pitch will be slow. The wavelength will be more spread out. **Day 4:** 1. wild animals; 2. Agriculture began and people started to grow crops. 3. Irrigation practices improved.

Page 38
Answers will vary but should show the connection between the materials, sound waves, and various pitches.

Page 39
Day 1: 1. 92, 105, 118, 131, 144; 2. 10; 3. 6,160; 4. 15;
Day 2: 1. short vowel sound; 2. timid, afraid;
3. B; 4. A; **Day 3:** Answers will vary.
Day 4: 1. Answers will vary but may include it is the separation of powers of the government so that no one branch becomes too powerful. 2. judicial; 3. legislative; 4. executive

Page 40
Answers will vary but should reflect accurate research and revision.

Page 41
Day 1: 1. 345 centimeters; 2. <; 3. 1, 3, 5, 15, 25, 75; composite; 4. 8,008; **Day 2:** 1. (circled) hind, tiny; 2. (circled) injury; 3. stiff, tiny; 4. The hairs would hurt your skin or eyes.
Day 3: 1. stamen: makes the pollen for fertilization; 2. sepal: covers the flower buds; 3. petal: keeps the parts that make seeds safe; 4. pistil: makes the eggs that grow into seeds; **Day 4:** 1. Citizens with military training. 2. The Loyalists felt strong ties to Britain and still wanted to follow Britain's laws. The Patriots wanted a separate American nation and wanted to make their own laws.

Page 42
Answers will vary but should include reasons to support the student's opinion.

Page 43
Day 1: 1. 91; 2. 977,319; 3. 10; 4. 294 hours;
Day 2: 1. Both are invertebrates and both have special eyes. 2. He likes them and is interested in them. 3. Answers will vary. **Day 3:** 1. C; 2. E; 3. B; 4. D; 5. A; **Day 4:** 1. fake; 2. Answers will vary but may include that special inks are mixed to color paper money and there are security threads in the bills.

Page 44
Answers will vary but should include evidence of student reflection and research.

Page 45
Day 1: 1. 17 feet; 2. eight hundred forty-one thousand five hundred four; 3. 2,700; 4. 16 × 12 = 192; **Day 2:** 1. (circled) he; 2. friendly, likeable, easy to get along with; 3. Everyone seems to like Dan. 4. Yes, it says everyone seems to like him. **Day 3:** 1. heredity; 2. diversity; 3. species; 4. trait; 5. inherit; **Day 4:** 1. D; 2. B; 3. A; 4. C

Page 46
Answers will vary but should reflect adequate research and include reasons to support the student's opinion.

Page 47
Day 1: 1. $2; 2. 900; 3. 10; 4. >; **Day 2:** 1. (first letter of the following words underlined) parks, american, america; 2. C; 3. Ms. Rodriguez showed us a picture of Henry Hudson. 4. uniform; **Day 3:** 1. S; 2. S; 3. B; 4. B; 5. B; 6. S; **Day 4:** 1. T; 2. T; 3. T; 4. F

Page 48
Answers will vary but should be organized with paragraphs and headings and include accurate research.

Page 49

Day 1: 1. 1, 1, and 1; 2. 38 bags, 23 bags;

Day 2: 1. (circled) coin, collecting, countries, country, collecting, coins, coin, collectors; 2. the hobby of coin collecting; 3. When Americans started collecting coins (about 1840). 4. They were busy surviving and building a country. **Day 3:** 1. A behavior is the way a living thing acts. 2. Answers will vary but may include a dog wags its tail, a fish swims, an ant digs tunnels underground, and a human laughs. **Day 4:** 1. to claim or own an idea; 2. dried tree sap; 3. General Santa Anna

Page 50

Answers will vary but should include details to describe thoughts, feelings, and actions.

Page 51

Day 1: 1. 1,232; 2. 16 meters; 3. 0.33; 4. $5\frac{8}{8}$ or 6;

Day 2: 1. (circled) ewes; 2. puppies; 3. Answers will vary. **Day 3:** 1. energy; 2. sugar; 3. herbivore; 4. carnivore; 5. omnivore; **Day 4:** 1. 196 years; 2. They did not have pointed tops. 3. pottery and statues

Page 52

Answers will vary. Allow time for sharing poems and for revisions.

Page 53

Day 1: 1. $14\frac{4}{8}$; 2. 1, 2, 17, 34; composite; 3. star; 4. 52; **Day 2:** 1. (first letter of the following words underlined) parks, (lowercase strike through the first letter) Seat; 2. A; 3. I want to see Baltimore, Maryland, on the Chesapeake Bay. 4. daisies;

Day 3: 1. An ecosystem is made up of living and nonliving things in an environment. 2. Answers will vary but may include forest, pond, mud puddle, or backyard. 3. Answers will vary.

Day 4: 1. to ease or get rid of; 2. Answers will vary but may include park benches. 3. Answers will vary but may include you can reuse a plastic bag instead of throwing it out.

Page 54

Answers will vary but should be based on research and use facts and definitions to explain or inform.

Page 55

Day 1: 1. =; 2. 57; 3. 0.32; 4. $\frac{3}{3}$ = 1 pizza;

Day 2: 1. speed skating; 2. She is the only American woman to win five Olympic gold medals. 3. the United States; **Day 3:** 1. Bean Seed Growth; 3, 1, 4, 5, 2; **Day 4:** 1. Answers will vary.

Page 56

Answers will vary but should include dialogue in the narrative. Allow time for students to share their narratives.

Page 57

Day 1: 1. 132 pounds; 2. Check students' answers. **Day 2:** 1. She has five older brothers and sisters who were champion speed skaters. 2. She learned to skate early. 3. kind; 4. They encouraged her. **Day 3:** 1. C; 2. A; 3. D; 4. E; 5. B; **Day 4:** 1. The ground is frozen the whole year through. 2. Because of the cold and windy conditions. 3. They can drink water when the marshes and lakes melt.

Page 58

Answers will vary but should be based on research and use facts and definitions to explain or inform.

Answer Key

Page 59
Day 1: 1. $4 \times (\frac{1}{6})$; 2. 1, 2, 3, 5, 6, 9, 10, 15, 18, 30, 45, 90; composite; 3. <; **Day 2:** 1. She became the best woman speed skater in the world. 2. three; 3. 500 meters and 1,000 meters; **Day 3:** 1. Check students' labeling. 2. The diagram shows how Earth revolves around the sun, the moon revolves around Earth, and the moon and Earth both rotate. **Day 4:** 1. river; 2. peninsula; 3. ocean; 4. volcano

Page 60
Answers will vary but should include details to describe thoughts, feelings, or actions. Each should have a beginning, middle, and ending.

Page 61
Day 1: 1. 0.68; 2. $3\frac{2}{5}$; 3. 5,604; 4. >; **Day 2:** 1. She became famous. 2. To focus on other competitions. 3. Answers will vary. 4. Answers will vary. **Day 3:** 1. true; 2. false, It takes exactly $29\frac{1}{2}$ days for the moon to circle around Earth. 3. false, The moon reflects the sun's light. 4. true; **Day 4:** 1. explode or burst; 2. people were buried alive; 3. Artifacts help historians learn more about the history of the subjects they are studying.

Page 62
Answers will vary but should include details to describe thoughts, feelings, or actions.

Page 63
Day 1: 1. $\frac{27}{4} = 6\frac{3}{4}$; 2. 0.4; 3. 188,000; 4. $\frac{1}{6}$; **Day 2:** 1. I am; 2. switched, turned around; 3. brat; 4. Bart's babysitter; **Day 3:** 1. A mineral is nonliving solid matter found in nature. 2. The following phrases should have a P: how hard it is; how shiny it is; how it breaks; its color; if it is magnetic; **Day 4:** 1. D; 2. A; 3. B; 4. C

Page 64
Answers will vary but should include accurate facts and definitions. Reports should be organized with headings and illustrations. Allow time for students to share with classmates.

Page 65
Day 1: 1. 7 tents; 2. $\frac{1}{4}$ of a gallon; 3. 0.28; **Day 2:** 1. He is bored. 2. He misses his friend. 3. Answers will vary. 4. yes; **Day 3:** 1. Scientists study fossils to learn about organisms that lived long ago, how Earth has changed, and how organisms have adapted to changing environments. 2. Answers will vary but may include scientists can compare the fossils they find with the animals living today. If the parts are the same, they can make inferences and draw conclusions that the animals looked and acted similarly. **Day 4:** 1. D; 2. B; 3. A; 4. C

Page 66
Answers will vary but should include details to describe thoughts, feelings, or actions. Allow time for sharing essays and for revisions.

Page 67
Day 1: 1. 3; 2. 47 pieces; 3. $6 \times (\frac{1}{6})$; **Day 2:** 1. percent, lysine, acid; 2. yummy, delicious, tasty; nutritious, healthful; 3. 60 to 70 percent protein; 4. to inform you; **Day 3:** 1. Deposition; 2. slows; 3. nutrients; 4. dunes; 5. beaches; 6. delta; **Day 4:** 1. 90° N; 2. equator; 3. southern

Page 68
Answers will vary but should include details and should give reasons to support opinions.

Page 69
Day 1: 1. 200, 300, 400, 500, 600, 700;
2. ⟷; 3. 538; **Day 2:** 1. (first letter of the following words underlined) the, north, states;
2. jog; 3. Benjamin Franklin said, "Early to bed and early to rise makes a man healthy, wealthy, and wise." 4. citizenship, imagination;
Day 3: 1. An earthquake is caused when the plates of the earth move, which makes the ground shake along a fault. 2. Answers will vary but may include an earthquake creates cracks in the earth. It causes human-made structures to fall. **Day 4:** 1. Prime Meridian; 2. eastern hemisphere; 3. western hemisphere

Page 70
Answers will vary but should include details to describe thoughts, feelings, or actions.

Page 71
Day 1: 1. Check students' answers; 2. 175°;
3. 21 books; **Day 2:** 1. stack, pile, ball; 2. female grasshoppers; 3. She lays eggs that will hatch in the spring. 4. no; **Day 3:** 1. The picture shows a warm front. A warm air mass is lighter and climbs over the heavier, colder air mass. The rising air cools and forms rain clouds.
Day 4: 1. western; 2. eastern; 3. western;
4. eastern; 5. eastern; 6. eastern

Page 72
Answers will vary but should include accurate facts and definitions. Reports should be organized with illustrations and headings.

Page 73
Day 1: 1. Students should have drawn four lines of symmetry; 2. 59; 3. right angle;
Day 2: 1. (first letter of the following words underlined) the, president, theodore, roosevelt;
2. goes; 3. "I am always doing that which I can not do in order that I may learn to do it," Pablo Picasso stated. 4. freedom, exploration;
Day 3: 1. water, evaporates, life, webs, climate, erode, sediment, rock; **Day 4:** 1. Answers will vary but may include they received better pay and working conditions. 2. He saw the hard work his family had to do in the fields.

Page 74
Answers will vary but should include details to describe the real or imaginary animal.

Page 75
Day 1: 1. 95°; 2. 8 × 4 = 32; 3. $\frac{4}{4}$ = 1 gallon;
Day 2: 1. not usual; 2. strange, weird, bizarre;
3. He has a painting that shows clocks melting.
4. B; **Day 3:** 1. the application of scientific knowledge to help people in many fields;
2. Answers will vary. **Day 4:** 1. Drawings will vary.

Page 76
Answers will vary but should include facts about the painting and the artist. It should conclude with the student's opinion of the artwork and include an illustration.

Page 77
Day 1: 1. 22°; 2. 21; 3. 123 r1; 4. 5 yards;
Day 2: 1. (circled) spaceship; 2. to be asleep;
3. They had not been awake since 2020.
4. one week's travel; **Day 3:** 1. Answers will vary but may include both engineers and scientists try to solve problems and follow a process. Engineers design things to solve problems, while scientists answer questions. Check students' underlining. **Day 4:** 1. Answers will vary but may include money. 2. Drawings will vary.

Page 78
Answers will vary but should include facts and definitions. Allow time for students to design a product brochure.

Page 79
Day 1: 1. 63°; 2. Yes, because all quadrilaterals and all squares have 4 sides. 3. 0.56;
Day 2: 1. It is a plant called a fungus; 2. spores that are in the air; 3. in warm, moist places; 4. fuzzy branches; **Day 3:** Answers will vary. 1. bread, cereal, pasta; 2. spinach, lettuce, peas; 3. apple, kiwi, orange; 4. yogurt, cheese, milk; 5. chicken, fish, beans; 6. nuts, avocados, olives; **Day 4:** 1. In times of distress. 2. In times of national mourning. 3. Answers will vary but may include that showing respect for a country's flag also shows respect for its citizens.

Page 80
Answers will vary but should include accurate facts and definitions. Reports should be organized with paragraphs and headings.

Page 81
Day 1: 1. 38°; 2. 1, 3, 29, 87; composite; 3. 20 pounds; **Day 2:** 1. (first letter of the following words underlined) denver, remember; 2. I; 3. (filled circles) loaves, potatoes; . He; **Day 3:** 1. pollution; 2. land; 3. noise; 4. water; 5. Air; **Day 4:** 1. B; 2. C; 3. A; 4. D

Page 82
Answers will vary but should include details and show imagination.

Page 83
Day 1: 1. 1,631; 2. <; 3. $1\frac{2}{8} = 1\frac{1}{4}$; 4. 400,000; **Day 2:** 1. features; 2. attract; 3. (circled) tend to, may try; 4. imaginary; **Day 3:** 1. The picture shows that some of the sun's heat is reflected off the ground. It strikes the heavy layer of gases and reflects back to Earth, where it is absorbed, instead of escaping into space.

2. The result is more heat and increased temperatures. **Day 4:** 1. Answers will vary.

Page 84
Answers will vary but should include details and dialogue.

Page 85
Day 1: 1. $1\frac{3}{4}$ miles; 2. $35\frac{3}{4}$ miles; **Day 2:** 1. He found new uses for peanuts and helped farmers; 2. Answers will vary; 3. Answers will vary. **Day 3:** 1. A natural resource is something found in nature that is useful. 2. The following items should have an R: air, cow, corn, rock, water, coal; **Day 4:** 1. Answers will vary.

Page 86
Reports will vary but should be based on research and include facts and definitions to explain or inform.

Page 87
Day 1: 1. 25,200; 2. 345; 3. $\frac{1}{12}$; 4. trapezoid, quadrilateral; **Day 2:** 1. (first letter of the following words underlined) one, nazi, jewish; 2. He; 3. monkeys, branches, . They; **Day 3:** 1. conservation; 2. extinct; 3. endangered; 4. protect; 5. refuge; **Day 4:** 1. Time lines will vary.

Page 88
Check students' time lines. Answers will vary but should include details to describe thoughts, feelings, or actions.

CD-104821 • © Carson-Dellosa